SEW & SERGE

PILLOWS!
PILLOWS!
PILLOWS!

OTHER BOOKS
AVAILABLE FROM CHILTON
Robbie Fanning, Series Editor

Contemporary Quilting

All Quilt Blocks Are Not Square, by Debra Wagner
Barbara Johannah's Crystal Piecing
The Complete Book of Machine Quilting, Second Edition,
    by Robbie and Tony Fanning
Contemporary Quilting Techniques, by Pat Cairns
Creative Triangles for Quilters, by Janet B. Elwin
Fast Patch, by Anita Hallock
Precision Pieced Quilts Using the Foundation Method,
    by Jane Hall and Dixie Haywood
The Quilter's Guide to Rotary Cutting, by Donna Poster
Scrap Quilts Using Fast Patch, by Anita Hallock
Stars Galore and Even More, by Donna Poster
Stitch 'n' Quilt, by Kathleen Eaton
Super Simple Quilts, by Kathleen Eaton
Three-Dimensional Pieced Quilts, by Jodie Davis

Craft Kaleidoscope

The Banner Book, Ruth Ann Lowery
The Crafter's Guide to Glues, by Tammy Young
Creating and Crafting Dolls, by Eloise Piper and Mary Dilligan
Fabric Crafts and Other Fun with Kids,
    by Susan Parker Beck and Charlou Lunsford
Quick and Easy Ways with Ribbon, by Ceci Johnson
Learn Bearmaking, by Judi Maddigan
Stamping Made Easy, by Nancy Ward

Creative Machine Arts

ABCs of Serging, by Tammy Young and Lori Bottom
Affordable Heirlooms, by Edna Powers and Gaye Kriegel
Alphabet Stitchery by Hand & Machine,
    by Carolyn Vosburg Hall
The Button Lover's Book, by Marilyn Green
Claire Shaeffer's Fabric Sewing Guide
The Complete Book of Machine Embroidery,
    by Robbie and Tony Fanning
Craft an Elegant Wedding,
    by Tammy Young and Naomi Baker
Distinctive Serger Gifts and Crafts,
    by Naomi Baker and Tammy Young
Gail Brown's All-New Instant Interiors
Hold It! How to Sew Bags, Totes, Duffels, Pouches, and More,
    by Nancy Restuccia
How to Make Soft Jewelry, by Jackie Dodson

Innovative Serging, by Gail Brown and Tammy Young
The New Creative Serging Illustrated,
    by Pati Palmer, Gail Brown, and Sue Green
A New Serge in Wearable Art, by Ann Boyce
Quick Napkin Creations, by Gail Brown
Second Stitches: Recycle as You Sew, by Susan Parker
Serge a Simple Project, by Tammy Young and Naomi Baker
Serge Something Super for Your Kids, by Cindy Cummins
Sew Any Patch Pocket, by Claire Shaeffer
Sew Any Set-In Pocket, by Claire Shaeffer
Sew Sensational Gifts, by Naomi Baker and Tammy Young
Sewing and Collecting Vintage Fashions,
    by Eileen MacIntosh
Shirley Botsford's Daddy's Ties
Simply Serge Any Fabric, by Naomi Baker and Tammy Young
Soft Gardens: Make Flowers with Your Sewing Machine,
    by Yvonne Perez-Collins
The Stretch & Sew Guide to Sewing Knits, by Ann Person
Twenty Easy Machine-Made Rugs, by Jackie Dodson

Know Your Serger Series,
by Tammy Young and Naomi Baker

Know Your baby lock

Sew & Serge Series,
by Jackie Dodson and Jan Saunders

Sew & Serge Pillows! Pillows! Pillows!
Sew & Serge Terrific Textures

StarWear

Dazzle, by Linda Fry Kenzle
Embellishments, by Linda Fry Kenzle
Jan Saunders' Wardrobe Quick-Fixes
Make It Your Own, by Lori Bottom and Ronda Chaney
Mary Mulari's Garments with Style
A New Serge in Wearable Art, by Ann Boyce
Pattern-Free Fashions, by Mary Lee Trees Cole
Shirley Adams' Belt Bazaar
Sweatshirts with Style, by Mary Mulari

Teach Yourself to Sew Better,
by Jan Saunders

A Step-by-Step Guide to Your New Home
A Step-by-Step Guide to Your Sewing Machine

SEW & SERGE

PILLOWS!
PILLOWS!
PILLOWS!

Jackie Dodson
Jan Saunders

Chilton Book Company
Radnor, Pennsylvania

Published in Radnor, Pennsylvania 19089, by Chilton Book
Company

Designed by Publication Design
Photography by Wyckoff Commercial

Manufactured in the United States of America

Library of Congress Cataloging in Publication Data

Dodson, Jackie.
    Pillows! pillows! pillows! / Jackie Dodson, Jan Saunders.
       p. cm. — (Sew & serge)
    Includes index.
    ISNB 0-8019-8530-7 (pbk.)
    1. Pillows. 2. Serging. I. Saunders, Janice S. II. Title.
  III. Series.
TT410.D64 1996
  646.2'1—dc20   95-51159
                                      CIP

1 2 3 4 5 6 7 8 9 0 5 4 3 2 1 0 9 8 7 6

Contents

CHAPTER 4
Pillow Poetry and Fantasy
Nine One-of-a-Kind Pillows to Keep or Give Away

CHAPTER 5
Way Past Plain
Professional Pointers for Producing Pillow Personality

CHAPTER 6
The Pillow Primer
Provisions and Procedures for Praiseworthy Pillows

Foreword

If you think the definition of a pillow is limited to two squares of fabric sewn together and stuffed through an opening, *Pillows! Pillows! Pillows!* will make you see pillows in a whole new fashion.

Jackie and Jan have collected a wonderful variety of pillow ideas in this book. Thanks to their clear instructions and innovative techniques, many of the projects are time-conserving (not consuming). Yet the finished products look classy, unique, and professional. It's encouraging that such great looking pillows do not require hours and hours of valuable sewing and creating time.

Turn to any page to check out the clever pillow possibilities from the authors and their sewing industry friends. They've convinced me that I will enjoy the process of making a small-scale piece of "art" to improve my pillow-less sofa. Besides that, I know that one of the pillow projects (maybe "Stack, Slash, and Bloom") will be chosen for our annual post-Christmas sewing party and another for a sewing day with my young nephew Matt, who'll love the pillow story stones. Talk about fun!

PHOTO COURTESY OF G.W. TUCKER

Mary Mulari
Teacher and author of
Sweatshirts with Style
and other creative sewing books

What is the *Sew & Serge* book series?

Pillows! Pillows! Pillows! is one of the kickoff books in our new *Sew & Serge* series. (*Sew & Serge Terrific Textures* is the other.) We hope you'll be inspired by the many ideas and new applications we've discovered during our brainstorming, research, and writing process. We also hope you'll love the exciting, cutting-edge techniques our top industry designers contributed to our efforts.

We work with the sewing machine and serger in tandem, because it shortens construction time, makes us more efficient (it's like using the microwave and conventional oven in cooking), and gives us two creative mediums to work in. But we also know that not everyone has a serger, so our instructions are written for both pieces of equipment (similar to recipes and instructions for preparing convenience foods with the conventional and microwave ovens).

We use icons to indicate which machine (if any) is needed for each project. This icon means the project or technique requires a serger, this icon means a sewing machine will be needed, and this icon **SEW** means neither machine is required. If the technique or project can be done with either machine, then both icons are listed: or .

The *Sew & Serge* books are filled with ideas, inspirations, and easy-to-do projects. In fact, we've organized our "easy, easier, and easiest" projects so that the easiest one in each chapter comes first. That way, you can sample a technique or concept with a minimum of time and effort. We hope that, regardless of your skill level, you'll enjoy our *Sew & Serge* projects — not only because they fill a need for a gift or will help complete a room, enhance an occasion, or accent an outfit, but also because they're fun to make. We've tried to respect your budget and busy schedule by offering projects that can be completed in one sitting. We've also been careful to give you the best way to create a project or stitch a technique, rather than including methods just because they're possible. If you like to explore short subjects in greater depth, as we do, give the *Sew & Serge* approach a try.

As we continue our creative adventures, we'd like to hear from you. Do you have an idea for a short subject sewing or crafting book? Or a sewing or crafting tip that you would like to share? Write to us in care of *Sew & Serge* development: 934 Meadow Crest Road, La Grange Park, IL 60525.

Acknowledgments

Thank you to the people who supplied us with fabulous fabrics: Lucille Tatulli and Pati Moses from Concord House; Nan Harding and Beth Touey from Fabric Traditions; Gary Fluxgold from Mill Creek Fabrics; Robin Steele and Nancy Walsh from V.I.P. Fabrics. Many thanks to Catherine Schieffer and Victoria Waller for providing beautiful decorator trims and their expert advice; to Emma Graham from The Crowning Touch; to Bonnie Benson from Quilters' Resource Inc.; and to Joyce Drexler of Sulky of America, who helped us decorate our pillows creatively.

And though you don't see them, their pillow forms made our pillows plump, and the designs look better — thank you to Air-Lite Synthetics Mfg., Inc.; Fairfield Processing Corp.; Morning Glory Products; and Sterns Technical Textiles Co.

Thank you, Gail Brown, for your idea on the Designer's Showcase. Just a phone call away, you're always available to listen, advise, help, and be a good friend to both of us. And to the designers who contributed so generously of their time, talent, and materials (and broke speed records making pillows and getting them to us), our thanks to the following: Donna Babylon, Naomi Baker, Sandra Benfield, Lynette Ranney Black, Gail Brown, Ann Bulgrin, Janis Bullis, Winky Cherry, Clotilde, Joyce Drexler, Shirley J. Fomby, Dianne Giancola, Caryl Rae Hancock, Maureen Kline, Melissa Palmer, Donna Salyers, Jane Schenck, Annie Tuley, Susan Voigt-Reising, Victoria Waller, Linda Wisner, Tammy Young, and Nancy Zieman.

Thank you, Susan Keller, for your attention to detail and everyone else at Chilton for your infinite patience.

Thank you, Robbie Fanning, our editor, for keeping us busy, sane, and for always convincing us we can do anything.

And a great big thank you to our families, who may not have time to read this — they've taken over holidays and other household jobs for us so we can sew, serge, and write.

Preface

Can we talk. . .pillows, that is? Pillows participate in our lives. We lie on them, they prop us up when we read, they cushion our kids' falls, and we all sit on them from time to time. We even throw them in fights. Pillows comfort our dogs and cats, pamper crooked necks and aching feet, and are plumped to make someone feel loved. Pillows bear rings. They accent, decorate, and are sometimes more expensive than the couches they sit on. They come in purposeful doll and toy shapes. We use them as seat cushions and flotation devices on boats and airplanes. They add color and comfort to patios and back decks, and are used as boosters to bring little ones up to the right height at family get-togethers. Pillows protect our knees when we plant and weed, and comfort us when we pray. So is there any wonder why there's so much to talk about?

Pillows are palettes on which we experiment with shape, texture, color, and technique. Once the inspiration hits, a spectacular pillow can be made in one sitting. Our pillows are designed to be made easily, with the easiest versions at the beginning of the book. Within each chapter, the easiest pillows are at the beginning of the chapter.

We know many readers have both a sewing machine and a serger so we suggest the most efficient pillow decorating and finishing techniques utilizing both. Instructions are also written so you don't have to rethink for the correct serge-order. If you don't have a serger, you can make any pillow in this book using more traditional techniques with your sewing machine. All of the techniques used and the machine needed for each are listed in the Pillow Parameters Box at the beginning of each project. If you need a serger to create a certain effect, the technique will be listed with this icon ⟨icon⟩ next to it. If you need a sewing machine, you'll see this: ⟨icon⟩. If either machine can be used, the icons will be shown in combination: ⟨icon⟩ or ⟨icon⟩. If you don't have a sewing machine, look for the attractive no-sew alternatives identified with this icon: ⟨SEW⟩.

The Pillow Parameters Box also tells you what type of pillow the project involves. Is it a cover for an existing pillow? A stuffed pillow made from scratch? A pillow created using a pillow form? Be sure to read "Pillow Forms and Other 'Stuff'" on page 67 for more information.

Most of our pillows have a purpose — decoration is always one, but other purposes include: to sleep and dream, to sit and look at, to play with, and sometimes to chuckle at. Find the chapter you like best:

- Don't have a lot of time or sewing knowledge? Then read about no-sew and quick-to-sew pillows in Chapter One: Poof! Pillows in an Instant.

- Have a beautiful scrap of fabric but not enough for a traditional pillow cover? Then read how to stretch it in Chapter Two: Peek-A-Boo Slipcover Pillows.

- Looking for something different and easy to make? Find pillows made from one triangle, two squares, a rectangle pinwheel, and more in Chapter Three: Playful Pillow Shapes and Surfaces.

- Need a beautiful pillow for a wedding, shower gift, or to help you to sleep a little better; want to comfort a child with a fun, soft companion? Then delight in the virtual plethora of Pillow Poetry and Fantasy in Chapter Four.

- Want new ideas for one of a kind pillows? The Professional Pointers for Producing Pillow Personality in Chapter Five will show you many creative ways to decorate your pillows using couching, fabric tubes, flatlocking, piping, ruffles, and pleats. Learn all about decorator trims, including terms and easy application tips; see just how easy it is to use your sewing machine or your serger to create shirring; and discover quilting shortcuts that will make your pillow projects a snap.

- Looking for a complete guide to pillow construction techniques? The Pillow Primer in Chapter Six reviews basic to professional pillow construction shortcuts, so choose the method you like best for each pillow, depending on your available time and materials. Also find the best tools and notions; see no-sew and easy-sew closures; find tips on making better buttonholes and the straightest edge-stitching; and learn techniques that apply not only to pillow-making but your other sewing and decorating projects as well.

- See what your favorite home decorating and sewing industry pros use to personalize their pillows by looking at the Designer Showcase in the color pages and in the Designer Showcase Key.

We hope *Pillows! Pillows! Pillows!* inspires you not only to make pillows! that you'll love and others will talk about, but also to have fun creating in the process. Enough talk. Let's make something.

Pleasant pillow-making,
J. D. and J. S.

SEW & SERGE

PILLOWS!
PILLOWS!
PILLOWS!

Chapter 1

POOF! PILLOWS IN AN INSTANT

Seven Pillows to Make When You're Pressed for Time

Need a new look for a room in your house. . . but have no time to dream it up? We hope these ideas give you instant inspiration. Use bandanas or suede and leather fringe for easy-to-make western flair. Attach hand-woven belting to a ready-made pillow to give it Guatemalan pizzazz. Decorate an embroidered dresser scarf with tassels for an elegant pillow which will dress up any room, or create a charmingly ruffled pillow for a country style. And make our Christmas pillow to bring extra holiday cheer into your home.

NO-SEW BANDANA PILLOWS

Here are two variations for this easy-to-make pillow.

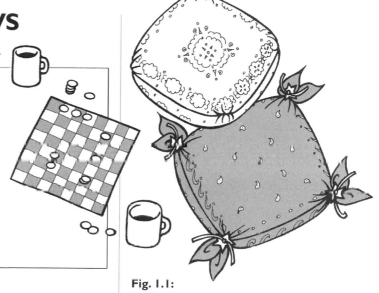

PILLOW PARAMETERS

PILLOW TYPE: **Pillow Made with Pillow Form**
(**Optional: Cover for existing pillow**)

PILLOW TECHNIQUES:

Measure It: Pillow Dimension Guidelines . . . . . p. 89

Pillow Forms and Other "Stuff" . . . . p. 67

~~SEW~~ Lacing and Rubber Band as Closures

~~SEW~~ Attaching Decorations by Tying

Fig. 1.1:
No-Sew Bandana Pillows.

You'll Need:

Fabric:

- Two bandanas per pillow

Miscellaneous:

- 16" (40.5cm) square pillow form per pillow
- Four conchos
- 48" (122cm) leather lacing (available in craft stores) for one pillow
- Four small rubber bands for each pillow

Rubber Band the Corners

1. On your work table, place two bandanas right sides together.

2. Slip bandana corners into small rubber bands.

3. Pull the corners through the rubber bands about 6" (15cm).

4. Turn bandanas right side out and slip in the pillow form. Adjust corners until the bandana fits snugly around the pillow form.

Conchos In the Corners

1. Sandwich the pillow form between two bandanas so the right sides of the bandanas are out. Rubber band the corners to keep the pillow form covered and the bandanas tight to the form.

2. Cut leather lace into four pieces. Tie one lace around each rubber band and pull through a concho.

3. Tie off laces, using a square knot to keep concho in place.

   VARIATIONS: *Use napkin or fabric squares over existing pillows to coordinate with your decor or holiday decorating scheme. When the holiday is over, remove the temporary cover (Fig. 1.2).*

Fig. 1.2:
Cover existing pillows with holiday no sew covers.

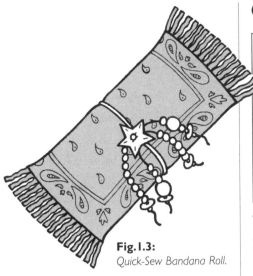

Fig.1.3:
Quick-Sew Bandana Roll.

QUICK-SEW BANDANA ROLL

PILLOW PARAMETERS

PILLOW TYPE: **Pillow Stuffed with Batting**

PILLOW TECHNIQUES:

Pillow Forms and Other "Stuff" . . . . p. 67

Attaching Decorations by Tying

Flatlocking Most Fabulous (optional) . . . . p. 61

You'll Need:

Fabric:

- One bandana

Thread:

- All-purpose to match bandana or monofilament

Miscellaneous:

- Two pieces of batting (the width of bandana minus 4" [10cm] × about 25" [63.5cm] or long enough so when the batting is rolled up, the bandana covers the batting)
- leather lacing or black soutache 48" (122cm) long
- one concho
- several pony beads (lacing, concho, and pony beads are available in craft stores)

Pillow Progression

1. Roll up batting pieces to fit inside the bandana (wrap bandana over the roll to measure).

2. Take off the bandana, place right sides together, and serge or sew the long sides creating a tube. Turn tube right side out.

3. Pull the roll of batting into the bandana tube, then sew or flatlock across the ends to close the pillow, leaving 2" (5cm) borders (Fig. 1.4). Cut 1½" long (4cm) fringe on both ends.

4. Tie a leather lace or braid around the middle and through a concho, pulling the lace tight. Add beads to the ends of the laces.

   VARIATIONS: *Look in the Designer Showcase Key and on the color pages to see what Jane Schenck from Pellon did with her Quilted Neck Roll Pillow.*

Fig.1.4: *Pull the roll of batting into tube; sew across ends and fringe.*

WOVEN GUATEMALAN BELTING PILLOW

POMPONS

PILLOW PARAMETERS

PILLOW TYPE: **Decoration for Existing Pillow**

PILLOW TECHNIQUES:

Measure It: Pillow Dimension Guidelines .... p. 69

 Attaching Decorations with Glue

 OR **Fabric Tubes Made Fast and Fun** .... p. 59

Fig. 1.5: *Woven Guatemalan Belting Pillow.*

You'll Need:

Fabric:
- 6 $\frac{1}{2}$ yards (6m) belting cut into six pieces

Thread:
- Monofilament

Miscellaneous:
- Nine pompons
- Hook-and-loop fastener
- 18" (46cm) ready-made chintz pillow to coordinate with belting
- Seam sealant
- Permanent washable glue

Pillow Progression

1. After cutting the belting into six pieces, brush the ends with seam sealant and let it dry. Then stitch hook-and-loop fastener at each end of the belting to create six loops.

2. Open the loops and weave the strips together over the pillow. Pin intersections.

3. Glue or machine-tack (with a wide zigzag stitch set at 0 length) the weaving at each pin.

4. Place weaving back on the pillow and press the hook-and-loop fastener together (Fig. 1.6). Dip pompons into glue and press them down at the intersections over your stitching.

VARIATIONS: *Guatemalan belting is available by the yard. You may also use ribbons or make fabric tubes to weave over the pillow (see Pillow Parameters Box).*

Fig. 1.6: *Weave belting, then glue or machine-tack. Add pompons and hook-and-loop fastener; then strap onto ready-made pillow.*

HOOK-AND-LOOP FASTENER

ANTIQUE LINEN ELEGANCE PILLOW

PILLOW PARAMETERS

PILLOW TYPE: **Pillow with Batting as Pillow Form**
PILLOW TECHNIQUES:

Fig. 1.7: *Antique Linen Elegance Pillow.*

You'll Need:

Fabric:
- One embroidered linen dresser scarf
- Plain fabric to cover batting for pillow form

Thread:
- All-purpose

Miscellaneous:
- Air-soluble marker
- Hook-and-loop fastener   • Permanent washable glue
- Three rayon chair cushion ties with tassels (available in home decorating departments of craft and fabric stores)
- Batting: roll and cut flat pad of batting three to four layers thick to fit odd-shaped linen (our finished pillow is 15" [38cm] square)

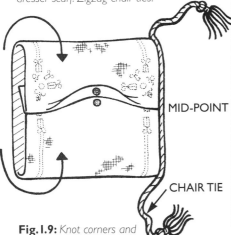

Fig. 1.8: *Fold, pin, stitch, and stuff an antique dresser scarf. Zigzag chair ties.*

MID-POINT

CHAIR TIE

Pillow Progression

1. Fold dresser scarf into an envelope to take advantage of the embroidery design. Mark overlap placement and stitch hook-and-loop fastener under the embroidery at the center front so it closes like an envelope.

2. Fold inside out, pin, and sew or serge down both sides. Turn right side out and press. *Note:* If the linen has a straight finished side, skip this step and proceed to the next.

3. Find the center of two chair ties and center of pillow sides and mark each. Match marks and apply cord. (Using a medium width, medium length zigzag and your embroidery foot, place the cord against the edge of the linen and zig on the cord, zag onto the linen, and so on.) Do not cut cord even with pillow corners (Fig. 1.8). Tie loops at top and bottom of the cord, if needed to match the length of the pillow side.

4. Center the third chair tie over the closure and machine tack it with a wide zigzag stitch on 0 stitch length. Tie a bow with the ties (Fig. 1.9).

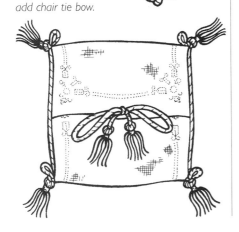

Fig. 1.9: *Knot corners and add chair tie bow.*

LEATHER RIBBON PILLOW

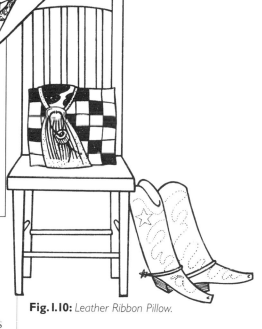

PILLOW PARAMETERS

PILLOW TYPE: **Pillow Made with Pillow Form**

PILLOW TECHNIQUES:

You'll Need:

Fabric:

- Purchased pillowcase, or ½ yard (1.5m) buffalo-check (looks like gingham check) flannel fabric
- Assortment of black, white, gray and red faux leathers and suedes
- Pony-print Ultrasuede 13" × 4½" (33cm × 11.5cm)
- Twelve white suede strips 13" (33cm) long
- Red leather lace 18" (46cm) long (leather and suede strips, and lacing are available at your local craft store)

Thread:

- All-purpose

Presser foot:

- Teflon for sewing leathers and suedes

Miscellaneous:

- 12" (30.5cm) square pillow form
- Concho beads

Pillow Progression

1. Open seams of purchased pillowcase and/or cut pillow top and back pieces large enough to fit your pillow form (see Pillow Parameters Box).

2. On pillow top, place the wide strip of red leather or suede slightly off-center. Using your Teflon presser foot, sew or serge across the top to secure the suede (Fig. 1.11).

3. Sew 12 white suede strips at the top back of the printed Ultrasuede; then center and sew or serge this onto the red suede (Fig. 1.12).

4. Tie the leather lace around the suedes 5" (12.5cm) from the top edge. Slip the leather lace through the concho and tie with a square knot. Cut pony-print Ultrasuede into long fringe below the tie (Fig. 1.13).

5. Smooth the red leather over the pillow front and baste it to the bottom of the pillow front. Create an envelope back for your pillow (see Pillow Parameters Box). Then, with right sides together, sew or

Fig. I.10: *Leather Ribbon Pillow.*

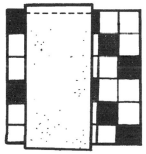

Fig. I.11: *Stitch wide leather strip to top of pillow.*

Fig. I.12: *Sew fringe and pony suede on top of leather strip.*

Fig. I.13: *Secure lacing around suedes with concho, fringe the pony suede, then smooth and attach leather strip to bottom of square.*

serge the pillow cover together. Turn cover right side out and insert the pillow form. Add beads and knots on the leather laces.

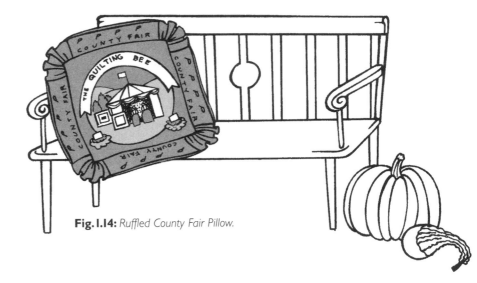

Fig. 1.14: *Ruffled County Fair Pillow.*

RUFFLED COUNTY FAIR PILLOW

PILLOW PARAMETERS

PILLOW TYPE: **Pillow Made with Pillow Form**

PILLOW TECHNIQUES:

You'll Need:

Fabric:

- One pillow panel (we used one from Concord's County Fair Collection)
- Four "County Fair" strips from the selvage edge cut 12" × 4" (33cm × 10cm)
- One yard (.9m) plain muslin

Thread:

- All-purpose

Miscellaneous:

- Three yards (2.8m) 1/2" (13mm) twisted polyester cable (upholstery) cord
- Three yards (2.8m) filler cord for gathering (pearl cotton, fishing line, or carpet and button thread)
- Pillow form to fit fabric panel (see Pillow Parameters Box)

Pillow Progression

1. Cut four 12" x 4" (30.5cm x 10cm) strips of muslin. Alternate and sew or serge "County Fair" and plain muslin strips together end-to-end (Fig. 1.15). Cut and piece another plain muslin strip to make it 90" x 4" (225cm x 10cm). Sew or serge both long strips together the long way to create a double-wide ruffle. Press seam open or to one side; then sew or serge this long strip into a loop.

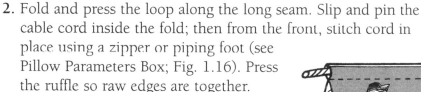

Fig. 1.15. *Alternate strips and join end to end.*

2. Fold and press the loop along the long seam. Slip and pin the cable cord inside the fold; then from the front, stitch cord in place using a zipper or piping foot (see Pillow Parameters Box; Fig. 1.16). Press the ruffle so raw edges are together.

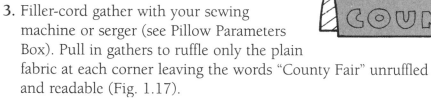

Fig. 1.16: *Stitch cable cord at the ruffle fold.*

3. Filler-cord gather with your sewing machine or serger (see Pillow Parameters Box). Pull in gathers to ruffle only the plain fabric at each corner leaving the words "County Fair" unruffled and readable (Fig. 1.17).

4. Cut out backing from the plain muslin and finish the pillow back, making the basic envelope (see Pillow Parameters Box).

VARIATIONS: *Use stripes, borders, and other pillow-panel coordinates to create this ruffle or to piece together creating a unique center medallion. Add some ribbon, a button, and tassel for decorated elegance (see Victoria Waller's pillow in the color insert and in the Designer Showcase Key).*

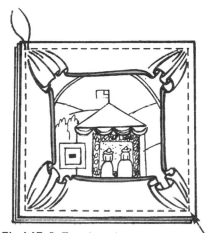

Fig. 1.17: *Ruffle only at the corners.*

GATHER
ONLY AT
CORNERS

WOOLEN FRINGED PILLOW

PILLOW PARAMETERS

PILLOW TYPE: **Pillow Made with Pillow Form**

PILLOW TECHNIQUES:

- (SEW) **Measure It: Pillow Dimension Guidelines** . . p. 69
- (SEW) **Pillow Forms and Other "Stuff"** . . . . p. 67
- (SEW) **Creating Self-fringe**
- OR **Envelop It: Making the Basic Envelope** . . . . p. 70

Fig. 1.18: *Woolen Fringed Pillow.*

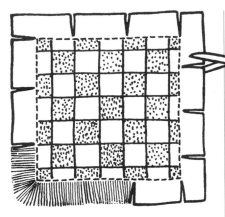

Fig. 1.19: *Clip every 3 - 4" (7.5 - 10cm), then pull out shorter crossgrain threads for easy fringing.*

You'll Need:

Fabric:
- 44" x 20" (111.5cm x 51cm) checked, loosely woven acrylic

Thread:
- Monofilament

Miscellaneous:
- 15" (38cm) pillow form
- Coordinating chair tie with tassels
- Decorative button

Pillow Progression

1. Cut a 20" (51cm) square for pillow front; cut remaining rectangle in half so you have two 20" x 12" (51cm x 30.5cm) pieces for the pillow back (see "Envelop It" in Pillow Parameters Box).

2. Serge-finish long sides of two smaller rectangles. Overlap the two serged edges to fit on the 20" (51cm) square top. Stack pillow top and back pieces, wrong sides together.

3. Pin and stitch around four sides of the square, sewing 2" (5cm) from the raw edges. Create self-fringe on all four sides of the top and back up to the stitching lines (Fig. 1.19).

4. Add tassels and button, securing them with a few hand stitches.

   VARIATIONS: *Make your pillow out of polar fleece, then cut fringe flanges to within ¹/2" (1.3cm) of the stitching.*

Do you want to decorate a pillow but you don't have enough fabric? Then go onto Chapter Two and read about our Peek-A-Boo Slipcover Pillows.

Doodle Page

POSSIBLE PILLOW PROJECTS

Pillow I'd Like to Make	For What Room or Special Purpose?	Page #	Sketch of Pillow
1.			
2.			
3.			
4.			
5.			

Chapter 2

PEEK-A-BOO SLIPCOVER PILLOWS

Six Pillows to Create When You Don't Have Enough Fabric for a Whole Pillow

If price or time are obstacles, then consider making a pillow slipcover. Buy an inexpensive ready-made pillow and decorate it with a small piece of special fabric. Have only a few pieces of interesting fabric? Combine them to create smashing pillow covers.

POP-IN PILLOW COVER

PILLOW PARAMETERS

PILLOW TYPE: **Pillow Made with Pillow Form**
(Optional: **Cover for an existing pillow**)

PILLOW TECHNIQUES:

Measure It: Pillow Dimension Guidelines . . . . p. 69

Pillow Forms and Other "Stuff" . . . . p. 67

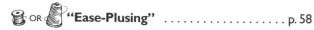 **"Ease-Plusing"** . . . . p. 58

Fig. 2.1: Pop-In Pillow Cover.

You'll Need:

Fabric:

- 28" (71cm) diameter circle of print fabric
- 14" (35.5cm) solid or coordinate fabric circle cut and pinked or serge-finished

Thread:

- All-purpose

Miscellaneous:

- 14" (35.5cm) round pop-in pillow form
- 1/4" (6mm) wide elastic; bodkin or ribbon threader
- Permanent washable glue
- Hand needle (optional)

Pillow Progression

1. Glue around edges or hand stitch small circle to one side of the pillow form, leaving about 3" (7.5cm) open.

2. Ease-stitch plus around the perimeter of the 28" (71cm) circle (see Pillow Parameters Box). If you ease-plus with your serger, remember when you chain off to give yourself enough chain to adjust the stitches.

3. To make the casing, fold ease-plused edge under 1/2" (1.3cm) and stitch, remembering to leave an opening to pull the elastic through. Thread elastic through the casing with a bodkin or ribbon threader and pull it up to fit around the form so the contrasting fabric circle shows.

Fig. 2.2: The Security Pillow. You can leave home without it.

VARIATIONS: *Put this slipcover around an existing covered pillow, or appliqué a little face, adding yarn bangs, that peeks out from the small circle through the opening. Jan's husband, Ted, suggested another variation on this pillow he calls The Security Pillow (Fig. 2.2). Before leaving home on vacation, tuck your valuables in behind the small circle and pop on the slipcover. Put it on the couch, smooth side out. "You can leave home without it!"*

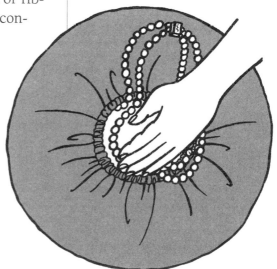

Fig. 2.3: *It's-A-Cinch Slipcover.*

IT'S-A-CINCH SLIPCOVER

You'll Need:

Fabric:

- One 44" × 12½" (111.5cm × 32cm) rectangle
- Two 14" (35.5cm) circles of coordinating fabric pinked or serge-finished

Thread:

- All-purpose

Miscellaneous:

- Permanent washable glue
- Hand needle (optional)
- 14" (35.5cm) round pop-in pillow form
- 2½ yards (2.3m) of 1½" (4cm) wide elastic shirring tape
- Matching ribbon or decorative cord

Pillow Progression

1. Glue around the edges or hand stitch to attach the smaller circles to opposite sides of the pillow form.

2. Fold and press ½" (1.3cm) hems along the long edges of the rectangular fabric. Following the manufacturer's instructions, attach the shirring tape to both long edges (Fig. 2.4; see Pillow Parameters Box).

Fig. 2.4: *Attach elastic shirring tape to both long edges.*

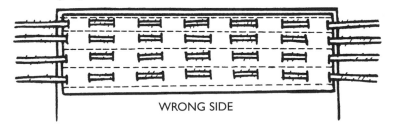

WRONG SIDE

3. Fold rectangle in half the short way, seaming it into a loop (Fig. 2.5) and being careful not to catch the shirring cords in the seam. Pull slipcover up around the pillow, adjusting gathers around the center opening (the pillow looks the same on both sides). Add ribbons or decorative cord to decorate.

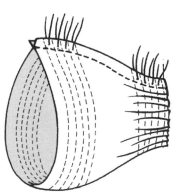

Fig. 2.5: *Seam strip into a tube, and pull elastic cords to cinch in the slipcover.*

STITCH-IT, STRAP-IT, BUTTON-ON BAG

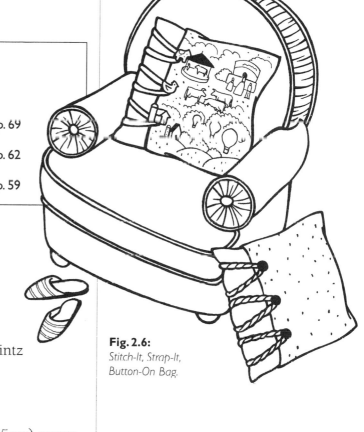

PILLOW PARAMETERS

PILLOW TYPE: **Decoration for Existing Pillow**

PILLOW TECHNIQUES:

Measure It: Pillow Dimension Guidelines . . . . p. 69

 **Quilting Quips (optional)** . . . . p. 62

OR **Fabric Tubes Made Fast and Fun** . . . . p. 59

You'll Need:

Fabric:

- One 34" × 20½" (86.5cm × 52cm) print

Thread:

- All-purpose

Miscellaneous:

- 18" (46cm) ready-made pillow covered in solid chintz to coordinate with print
- Seven decorative buttons

Pillow Progression

1. From the print fabric, cut a strip 2" × 34" (5cm × 86.5cm) across the grain. Fold it in half the long way, right sides together, and sew or serge it into a long tube using ¼" (6mm) seam allowances. Turn the tube right side out and press (for some shortcuts for fabric tubes, see Pillow Parameters Box).

2. Fold remaining rectangle in half the short way and serge or sew across the sides adjacent to the fold to create a bag. Overcast or serge-finish around the opening.

3. Fold a 2" (5cm) hem around the opening and topstitch around it 1½" (4cm) from the hem fold. Slip your pillow inside the bag.

   PILLOW POINTER: *For an evenly stitched wide hem, adjust your quilting guide out to hem fold (see Pillow Parameters Box).*

4. Pin the tube in place, zigzagging it back and forth across the opening as shown (Fig. 2.7). Turn under tube on the two free ends, cut off excess tubing, and sew a button to anchor each end. Hand or machine tack tubes so that the laced strap creates button loops for each button and so that the strap is more secure. Sew the other five buttons on so that the fabric tube buttons over them. This cover is easily removed for laundering.

   VARIATIONS: *If you have even less fabric, use lace, ribbon, or decorator trim as the lacing instead of making the fabric tube.*

Fig. 2.6:
*Stitch-It, Strap-It,
Button-On Bag.*

Fig. 2.7: *Stitch and hem the bag; zigzag and button-on fabric strap; tack the strap about 1" (2.5cm) from each bend to make large enough loops to button through.*

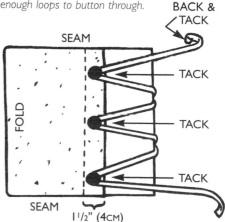

TUBE AND TIE SLIPCOVER

PILLOW PARAMETERS

PILLOW TYPE: Decoration for Existing Pillow

PILLOW TECHNIQUES:

Fig. 2.8: *Tube and Tie Slipcover*

You'll Need:

Fabric:

- One print rectangle and one solid rectangle, each cut 29" × 10" (73.5cm × 25.5cm)

Thread:

- All-purpose

Miscellaneous:

- 14" (35.5cm) ready-made pillow covered in coordinating solid 96" (2.5m) of 1/2"- (1.3cm) wide grosgrain ribbon cut into eight pieces of equal length

Pillow Progression

1. Pin four 1/2" (1.3cm) ribbons to each long side of print fabric, 3 3/4" (9.5cm) from the bottom and top at both sides, and 6 1/2" (16.5cm) apart for center ribbons (Fig. 2.9).

2. With right sides together, sew or serge print and solid fabrics together at the long edges with a 1/4" (6mm) seam allowance, and catching in the ribbons at the same time. Turn tube right side out and press.

3. To make this pillow slipcover reversible, put right sides of print fabric together and seam short ends with 1/4" (6mm) seam allowances to create a loop. Continue sewing 11/2"-2" (4cm - 5cm) into the solid fabric (Fig. 2.10). Close the rest of the opening by hand or edgestitch (see Pillow Parameters Box). If you don't want it to be reversible, put right sides of print fabric together and serge.

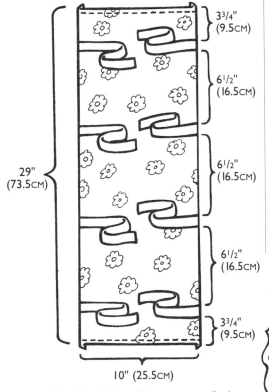

29" (73.5CM)

3 3/4" (9.5CM)

6 1/2" (16.5CM)

6 1/2" (16.5CM)

6 1/2" (16.5CM)

3 3/4" (9.5CM)

10" (25.5CM)

Fig. 2.9: *Position ribbons, narrow roll-edge the sides, seam into a tube, then tie onto a ready-made pillow.*

4. Slip the pillow into the fabric tube and tie the ribbons into bows.

VARIATIONS: *If you don't want to line the tube, serge a narrow rolled hem along the two long sides (see Pillow Parameters Box), serging the ribbons into the edges simultaneously.*

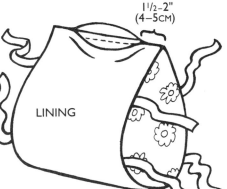

11/2–2" (4–5CM)

LINING

Fig. 2.10: *To make it reversible, position ribbons, place second rectangle on the first, right sides together, and finish.*

Top Row (left to right):
Pop-In Pillow Cover, *Chapter Two*; Woven Guatemalen Belting Pillow, *Chapter One*;
Lickety-Split Tie-On Squares, *Chapter Two*.
Middle Row (left to right):
No-Sew Bandana Pillow, *Chapter One*; It's-A-Cinch Slipcover, *Chapter Two*;
No-Sew Bandana Pillow, Chapter One, Bits and Pieces, *Chapter Two*.
Bottom Row (left to right):
Tube and Tie Slipcover, *Chapter Two*; Quick Sew Bandana Roll, *Chapter One*.

Top Row (left to right):
Ruffled County Fair Pillow, *Chapter One*;
Wipe-Clean Outdoor Pillow, *Chapter Three*; Stitch-It, Strap-It, Button-On Bag, *Chapter Two*.
Middle Row (left to right):
Leather Ribbon Pillow, *Chapter One*;
Woolen Fringed Pillow, *Chapter One*; Petal Pillow, *Chapter Three*.
Bottom Row (left to right):
Funny Faces Man, One-Square Pincushion, Funny Faces Dog,
and interchangeable parts for faces, Chapter Four.

Designer Showcase

Clockwise from upper left: Double Diagonal, *Donna Babylon;* Charted Needlework and Quilting, *Joyce Drexler;* Ultra-Pillow, *Nancy Zieman;* Ultrasuede Patchwork, *Linda Wisner;* Ultra-Pillow, *Nancy Zieman;* Easy and Elegant, *Gail Brown.*

Clockwise from upper left:
Wavy Circle, *Caryl Rae Hancock;*
Medallion Pillow, *Victoria Waller (in center);*
Scrapbasket, *Ann Bulgrin;*
Going Baroque, *Susan Voigt-Reising;*
Fringe Tapestry, *Lynette Ranney Black.*

For a detailed description of each texture shown, refer to the Designer Showcase Key at the back of the book.

Clockwise from upper left:
Quintessence, *Shirley J. Fomby;*
Decorative Tubes, *Sandra Benfield;*
Shirred Fun, *Janis Bullis;*
Quilted Neck Roll, *Jane Schenck;*
Ruffled Bow, *Naomi Baker and Tammy Young.*

Clockwise from upper left:
Dritz No-Sew Sunflower, *Janis Bullis;*
Annie Tuley's Twisted Ribbon, *Annie Tuley;*
Fabulous-Fur/Fabu-Leather, *Donna Salyers;*
Lion Pillow, *Maureen Klein;*
Melissa's Pillow, *Melissa Palmer;*
Pleated Churn Dash, *Annie Tuley.*

Top Row (left to right):
Stack, Slash, and Bloom Pillow, *Chapter Three;*
Two-Triangle Pillow, *Chapter Three;* Humbug Pillow, *Chapter Three.*
Middle Row (left to right):
Ote-Dama Pillow, *Chapter Three;*
Todd's Favorite One-Triangle Pillow, *Chapter Three;* Double-Square Pillow, *Chapter Three.*
Bottom Row (left to right):
Funny Faces Pillow, *Chapter Four;* Pillow Story Stones, *Chapter Four.*

Top Row (left to right):
Grandmother's Flower Garden Pillow, *Chapter Four;*
Tiny Battenburg Sleep Pillow, *Chapter Four;* Antique Linen Elegance Pillow, *Chapter One.*
Middle Row (left to right):
Heirloom Hanky Sleep Pillow, *Chapter Four;* Wedding Pillow, *Chapter Four;*
Jackie's Wedding Dress Sleep Pillow, *Chapter Four.*
Bottom Row (left to right):
Battenburg Sleep Pillows *(two children and a star),* Chapter Four;
Heirloom Sampler Sleep Pillow, *Chapter Four;*
Triangle Battenburg Sleep Pillow, *Chapter Four.*

LICKETY-SPLIT TIE-ON SQUARES

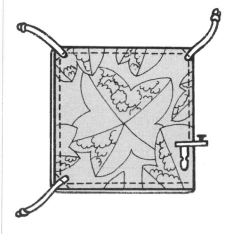

PILLOW PARAMETERS

PILLOW TYPE: **Decoration for Existing Pillow**

PILLOW TECHNIQUES:

Measure It: Pillow Dimension Guidelines . . . . . p. 69

Fig. 2.11: *Lickety-Split Tie-On Squares.*

You'll Need:

Fabric:
- Two 15" (38cm) squares of print
- Two 15" (38cm) squares of solid lining

Thread:
- All-purpose
- Monofilament

Miscellaneous:
- Hand needle
- 8" (20.5cm) strip of fusible web
- Permanent washable glue and a toothpick
- Two yards (1.85m) twisted cable (upholstery) cord
- 18" (46cm) square ready-made chintz-covered pillow
- Two yards (1.9m) welting (fabric-covered cable cord) to match your fabric

Pillow Progression

1. Place one print square and one lining square, right sides together. Repeat to make second square. Serge or sew all the way around each pair of squares using a ¼" (6mm) seam allowance.

2. Slit 4" (10cm) openings on the bias and in the middle of the each lining and turn squares right side out; press.

   PILLOW POINTER: *Make this pillow cover reversible by embellishing over lining slit with coordinating ribbon or trim.*

3. Cut cable (upholstery) cord in half. Starting in the middle of one side, pin one piece up inside one square, working the cord into the seam and pinning around the inside edges (Fig. 2.12). When cord ends meet, tape and cut the ends to butt up against each other (see page noted in Pillow Parameters Box for additional tips). Repeat for other square.

4. Nudge the zipper foot against the cord and stitch around the inside edge of each square (Fig. 2.13). Tuck a strip of fusible web under the slit and fuse it closed.

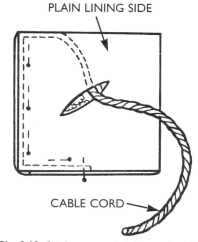

PLAIN LINING SIDE

CABLE CORD

Fig. 2.12: *Stitch square, slit lining on the bias and turn square through. Position cable cord around the inside perimeter and stitch.*

Fig. 2.13: *Add covered cord at each corner.*

5. Cut fabric-covered cord into eight pieces and tie overhand knots on one end of each. Stuff raw ends back into the knots with a toothpick. Push glue down into the knots to keep them in place. On the other end of each cord, pull out 1" (2.5cm) of filler cord and cut it off. Push the raw edge down into the cording and either hand stitch or glue the opening closed. Stitch flattened end at each corner of pillow cover and tie squares onto the ready-made pillow as shown.

VARIATIONS: *Attach cord or ribbon ties to two 15" (38cm) fabric squares or napkins. For a Secret Square pillow cover, make a 6" - 10" (15 - 25.5cm) long corded buttonhole sewn off-center and on the lengthwise grain (see Pillow Parameters Box). Cut buttonhole open and turn your squares. Now you have a secret pocket for a Teddy bear or to store pajamas—a great gift for any preschooler.*

BITS AND PIECES

PILLOW PARAMETERS

PILLOW TYPE: **Pillow Made with Pillow Form**
PILLOW TECHNIQUES:

You'll Need:

Fabric:
- ¹⁄₂ yard (46cm) crinkly cotton or cotton gauze;
- 16" × 36" (40.5 × .95m) ethnic cotton stripe

Thread:
- Monofilament
- All-purpose for buttonholes

Miscellaneous:
- 16" square pillow form
- Two yards (1.85m) ¹⁄₄" (6mm) twisted cable (upholstery) cord
- One yard (.95m) fine decorative cord
- Six beads with holes big enough for decorative cord
- 22" × 16" (56cm × 40.5cm) fusible knit interfacing

Fig. 2.14: *Bits and Pieces.*

Pillow Progression

1. Cut one 16" (40.5cm) square each of crinkly cotton and fusible knit interfacing. Following the manufacturer's instructions, fuse interfacing to the wrong side of the cotton.

2. Cut two 3" × 16" (7.5cm × 40.5cm) vertical stripes from ethnic cotton. Fold and press long edges under ¼" (6mm) or serge-finish with a narrow rolled hem (see Pillow Parameters Box).

3. Cut and interface one 5" × 16" (12.5cm × 40.5cm) piece so the stripes are parallel to the short side. Mark three sets of buttonholes as shown (Fig. 2.15). Stitch buttonholes with all-purpose thread and cut them open (see Pillow Parameters Box). *Note:* The striped fabric is cut in both directions to utilize the stripes and make a more interesting pillow.

4. Arrange the striped fabric on the crinkly cotton, overlapping the buttonhole strip with vertical-striped pieces, ¾" (2cm) on each side. Edgestitch along the fold or just inside the narrow rolled edges of striped pieces (see Pillow Parameters Box).

5. Cut remaining striped fabric into 1½" (4cm) strips, cutting them across the grain. Seam strips end to end, and cover the cable cord to make the piping. Attach piping to pillow front (see Pillow Parameters Box). Cut, stitch, and finish pillow back by making an envelope (see Pillow Parameters Box). Tie decorative cord around each pair of buttonholes to reveal solid crinkle cotton underneath; tie a bead to each cord end.

   VARIATIONS: *Rather than tying buttonholes together, weave a ribbon or other trim through the buttonholes before attaching the piping around the pillow. Cut belting the diameter of the pillow (or use a western belt), plus 2" (5cm) for overlap. Weave belt through the buttonholes; overlap and secure ends with hook-and-loop fastener. If you've used a real belt, buckle the ends. The buckle may look good as part of the pillow embellishment, too.*

Sometimes the fabric dictates the technique and pillow design. See how fabric inspiration is used to make pillows into different, playful shapes in Chapter Three.

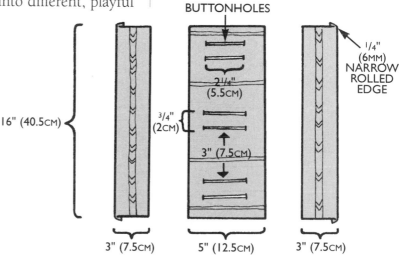

Fig. 2.15: *Cut, finish, and make buttonholes on ethnic stripe; then attach to solid pillow top.*

BUTTONHOLES

¼"
(6MM)
NARROW
ROLLED
EDGE

2¼"
(5.5CM)

¾"
(2CM)

3" (7.5CM)

16" (40.5CM)

3" (7.5CM)   5" (12.5CM)   3" (7.5CM)

PLAYFUL PILLOW SHAPES AND SURFACES

Nine Pillows for the Kid in You

We're all so used to standard square and round pillow shapes that we often don't think of buying or making anything else. Maybe you've tried a rectangular or bolster pillow but haven't gone much further than that. Let this chapter help you. You can use our "playful shapes" for a game of catch or make them extra large and fall into them for a comfortable landing. The other pillows in this chapter will help you see the many possibilities in a pillow's surface — from slick to layered to flowering fun!

PLAYFUL SHAPES

All of these pillows are based on geometric shapes. Included are one square, double squares, an equilateral triangle, double triangles, one rectangle (used to make a Humbug), and four rectangles (to make the Ote-dama). We found these pillows easier to understand and more fun to make when we made mini pillows from scraps first.

General Construction

1. For these pillows, use ½" (1.3cm) seam allowances except where noted. Follow the cutting and folding instructions for each pillow.

2. Add interesting fringes, piping, or fringe points to one seam.

3. With right sides together, sew or serge (using a wide 3/4-thread stitch) and leaving at least a 5" (12.5cm) opening.

4. Turn and stuff with loose fiberfill (see Pillow Parameters Box; we used at least one pound in each pillow).

5. Close the last side by edgestitching (see Pillow Parameters Box) or by hand-stitching.

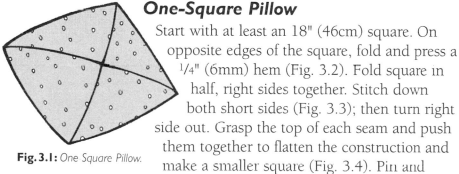

Fig. 3.1: *One Square Pillow.*

One-Square Pillow

Start with at least an 18" (46cm) square. On opposite edges of the square, fold and press a ¼" (6mm) hem (Fig. 3.2). Fold square in half, right sides together. Stitch down both short sides (Fig. 3.3); then turn right side out. Grasp the top of each seam and push them together to flatten the construction and make a smaller square (Fig. 3.4). Pin and edgestitch along folded edges from either end toward the center, leaving an opening. Stuff; then close by machine edgestitching (see Pillow Parameters Box) or by hand. Add tassels to the corners for a sensational pin cushion (see Pillow Parameters Box). Start with a bigger square for a fanciful throw pillow.

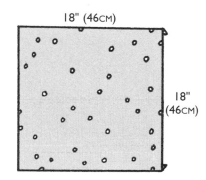

Fig. 3.2: *Fold and press a ¼" (6mm) hem on opposite edges of an 18" (46cm) square.*

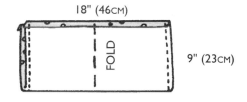

Fig. 3.3: *Stitch down both short sides. Fold and press.*

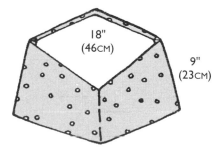

Fig. 3.4: *Grasp the top of each seam and push together.*

Fig.3.5: *Double-Square Pillow.*

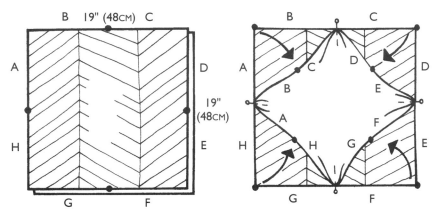

Double-Square Pillow

Cut two different fabrics, each 19" (48cm) square. Mark the center point of each straight edge of both squares. Mark square sides from letter A to H as shown (Fig. 3.6). Place one square over the other, right sides together, and rotate the top square counterclockwise so that the corner points are centered on the dots marked on the straight sides (Fig. 3.7). This creates slack, which provides the dimension for stuffing. Pin each corner. Fold the corners of the other square so that they touch in the center. Using 1/4" (6mm) seam allowances, sew or serge squares together leaving part of one side open for stuffing. Turn, stuff, then close by machine edgestitching (see Pillow Parameters Box) or by hand sewing.

Fig.3.6: *Cut two different fabric squares. Mark the center point of each side of each square, then label the sides.*

Fig.3.7: *Place one square over the other.*

Todd's Favorite One-Triangle Pillow

(Todd, Jan's seven-year-old son, was crushed when this pillow had to leave the house for photography, but he didn't mind its leaving if we named it after him.) Start with an equilateral triangle (each angle is 60 degrees, each side is the same length). We used 24" (61cm) sides. Mark sides of triangle (Fig. 3.9).

To make the fringe, laminate a 7" × 11" (18cm × 28cm) strip of matching fabric using fabric laminating film or paper-backed fusible web and following the manufacturer's instructions. Fold strip in half the long way and cut fringe from the folded edge to within 1/2" (1.3cm) of the cut edges of the strip.

Glue-stick fringe to the right side of side C as shown in Figure 3.9. Fold sides A, B, and C at their midpoints to form the triangle. The dashed line represents the base of the pillow. Pin along sides A and C and sew or serge them. Pin and sew or serge side B, leaving an opening for turning. Turn, stuff, and close by edgestitching (see Pillow Parameters Box) or by hand sewing.

Fig.3.8: *Todd's Favorite One-Triangle Pillow.*

Fig.3.9: *Cut an equilateral triangle and mark the sides.*

Two-Triangle Pillow

Using contrasting fabrics, cut two equilateral triangles (each side equal length; each angle 60 degrees). We used 24" (61cm) sides. Mark, fold, and pin sides, leaving slack as you did in the Double Square pillow (Fig. 3.11). Sew or serge sides, leaving an opening (Fig. 3.12). Turn, stuff, and then close by edgestitching (see Pillow Parameters Box) or by hand sewing.

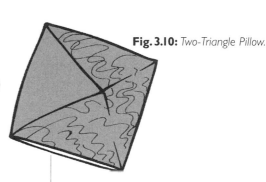

Fig. 3.10: *Two-Triangle Pillow.*

Fig. 3.11: *Mark the midpoint of each side of the two triangles.*

Fig. 3.12: *Put the triangles right sides together and rotate the top one so that its corners meet the midpoints of the bottom triangle.*

Humbug Pillow

This pillow is named after an English candy. Cut one rectangle 44" × 17" (111.5cm × 43cm) and mark it as shown (Fig. 3.14). Cut a strip of contrasting fabric 21" × 6½" (53.5cm × 16cm), fold it in half the long way, wrong sides together. Slip a strip of 21" × 3" (53.5cm × 7.5cm) fusible web inside the strip and fuse it together. Cut out points as shown (Fig 3.15). Center and sew this strip, right sides together to one 22" (56cm) side (see Fig. 3.15). Fold rectangle in half the short way and seam side A to side A to form a tube (Fig. 3.16). Refold so B and C marks are at the ends and seam that side closed (Fig. 3.17). Then fold so D and E are at the ends (Fig. 3.18). Stitch part way, leaving an opening. Turn, fill; then close by machine edgestitching (see Pillow Parameters Box) or by hand sewing.

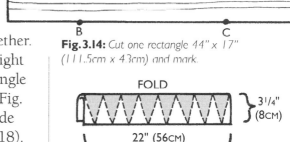

Fig. 3.14: *Cut one rectangle 44" × 17" (111.5cm × 43cm) and mark.*

Fig. 3.13: *Humbug Pillow.*

Fig. 3.15: *Cut out points.*

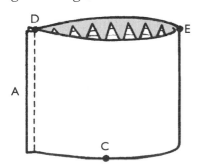

Fig. 3.16: *Fold rectangle in half and sew to form a tube.*

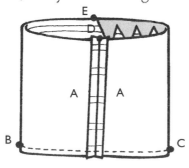

Fig. 3.17: *Refold so B and C marks are at the ends and seam that side closed.*

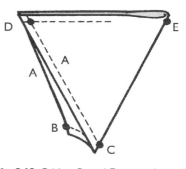

Fig. 3.18: *Fold so D and E are at the ends. Stitch, leaving an opening.*

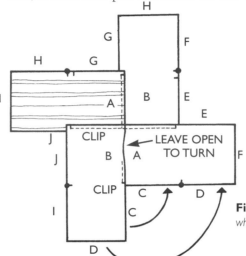

Fig. 3.19: *Ote-dama Pillow.*

Ote-dama Pillow

Cut four rectangles from contrasting fabric, each 9" × 18" (23cm × 46cm). Sew two rectangles together, stopping ¼" (6mm) from the top of rectangle A as shown (Fig. 3.20); repeat for the remaining rectangles. *Note:* If your machine has a locking stitch, use it at the end of each seam allowance to secure what will become the corners of this pillow. Press seams open or to one side. Join the four rectangles into a pinwheel shape (Fig. 3.21). Clip the seam allowance to the locking stitches. Mark the middle of each rectangle. Starting at one end, match and pin the sides all the way around turning rectangles around each corner at the clips. Stitch Ote-dama together, pivoting at each corner and leaving part of one side open. Turn, fill; then close by machine edgestitching (see Pillow Parameters Box) or by hand sewing.

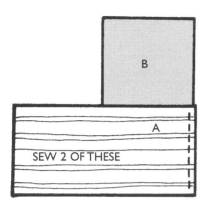

SEW 2 OF THESE

Fig. 3.20: *Cut four rectangles from contrasting fabric, each 9" x 18" (23cm x 46cm). Stitch two rectangles together, stopping ¹/4" (6mm) from the top and bottom of rectangle A.*

CLIP

LEAVE OPEN TO TURN

CLIP

Fig. 3.21: *Join the four rectangles into a pinwheel shape.*

Fig. 3.22:
Wipe-Clean Outdoor Pillow.

WIPE-CLEAN OUTDOOR PILLOW

We have enjoyed laminating almost any fabric with iron-on flexible vinyl. Simply remove the protective paper and smooth vinyl over the fabric, sticky side down. Place the protective paper, shiny side down on the vinyl, and press over the paper. To complete the bond, turn and press over the fabric side. Because there are several types of iron-on flexible vinyl on the market, always test on a scrap first following the manufacturer's instructions. "Vinylize" fabric for rainwear, make wipe-clean place mats, sew outdoor slipcovers, make waterproof tote bags...the possibilities are almost endless.

You'll Need:

Fabric:

- ½ yard (46cm) jungle print or one pre-printed pillow panel
- ¼ yard (23cm) each of two coordinate prints (we used companion rust and green prints from Concord)
- 2 yards (1.85m) iron-on flexible vinyl (this comes in 18" (46cm) widths and we are allowing extra for testing)

Thread:

- Monofilament

Needle:

- #80/12 sharp

Presser foot:

- Teflon

Miscellaneous:

- Iron
- 16" square pillow form
- See-through ruler
- Permanent marker
- Cardboard
- Ironing board
- Rotary cutter and board
- Glue stick
- Large Teflon pressing sheet or paper removed from the film
- 3" × 8" (7.5cm × 20.5cm) piece of cardboard for template

Pillow Progression

1. Cut a 17" (40.5cm) square of jungle print and iron-on flexible vinyl for pillow front, and fuse film to the right side of the print following the manufacturer's instructions. Cut jungle print to make an envelope closure for a 17" (40.5cm) pillow back (see Pillow Parameters Box). Pink around outside edges.

2. To create the quick-cut fringe points, fuse film or paper-backed fusible web to the underside of two rust strips. Cool, remove paper and fuse each rust strip to a green strip, wrong sides together, using the Teflon pressing sheet to protect your iron. Laminate entire strip with laminating film following manufacturer's instructions and using the Teflon pressing sheet, again to protect the iron.

3. Prepare a cardboard template (Fig. 3.23). Cut out edging from the vinylized strip using the template as a pattern. Glue-stick edging to the wrong side of fabric around the pillow front, under-

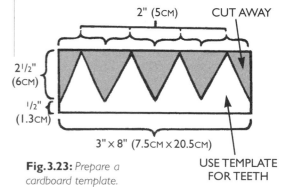

Fig. 3.23: *Prepare a cardboard template.*

2" (5cm) CUT AWAY

2½" (6cm)

½" (1.3cm)

3" × 8" (7.5cm × 20.5cm)

USE TEMPLATE FOR TEETH

Fig. 3.24: *Glue-stick edging to wrong side of fabric.*

lapping edging ¹/₂" (1.3cm). Piece the edging if necessary by butting the teeth next to each other and using your glue stick to hold them in place (Fig. 3.24).

4. Glue-stick front and back pillow pieces, *wrong sides together.* Stitch around all sides, following a presser foot width from pinked edge. Pop in pillow form and throw it on the front porch swing or back patio.

VARIATIONS: *Use the fabric laminating film to make any fabric "unravellable," then duplicate shapes in a print to create interesting borders, edges, three-dimensional prairie points, and appliqués.*

STACK, SLASH, AND BLOOM PILLOW

Blooming fabric is a clever embellishment that finds its way into fabric texturing and quilting. Here we use the pattern of the fabric as the basis for our "blooming" design.

PILLOW PARAMETERS
PILLOW TYPE: **Pillow Created Using Pillow Form**
PILLOW TECHNIQUES:
Measure It: Pillow Dimension Guidelines . . . . p. 69
Pillow Forms and Other "Stuff" . . . . p. 67

        Blooming Fabric

OR **Envelop It: Making the Basic Envelope** . . . . p. 70

OR **Attaching Welting Made from Cable Cord** . . . . p. 52

You'll Need:
Fabric:
- One 16" (40.5cm) 100% cotton striped fabric or print napkin
- Four 16" (40.5cm) 100% cotton fabric squares in solid colors to coordinate with print (we used green, yellow, peach, and red)

Thread:
- Monofilament

Miscellaneous:
- Ruler
- Disappearing marker   • Small clipping scissors
- 16" (40.5cm) square pillow form
- One package of color-coordinating pre-made welting (piping)

Pillow Progression
1. Mark stitching lines on the print fabric or napkin with the disappearing marker and ruler. We followed the zigzag stripes of our

Fig. 3.25: *Stack, Slash, and Bloom Pillow.*

fabric and marked the lines ³/₄" (2cm) apart in the center of the stripes because the stripes were uneven.

2. Layer three solid-colored fabrics under print. Pin layers together, and stitch on each marked line.

3. Clip halfway between the stitched lines through three layers (the top plus two solid fabrics), clipping the V's to the stitching line (Fig. 3.26). Don't cut through the bottom layer. Soak this piece in cold water, roll in a towel to extract most of the water, then dry in the dryer with a clean tennis ball or tennis shoes. The drying action of the ball or shoe bounces against the fabric to "bloom" the slashes.

4. Sew or serge welting around the perimeter of the bloomed square (see Pillow Parameters Box). Cut, assemble, and finish back envelope (see Pillow Parameters Box), turn right side out, then pop in the pillow form.

   VARIATIONS: *If you don't have a zigzag stripe for your pillow top, use a print and mark the zigzags ³/₄" to 1" (7.5cm to 10cm) apart, so each angle is on the bias.*

   SEW-HOW: *For variations on the blooming fabric technique, see Sew & Serge Terrific Textures (Chilton, 1996), our other volume in the Sew & Serge series.*

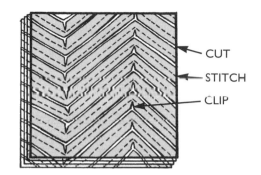

Fig. 3.26: *Clip halfway between the stitch lines through three layers, clipping the V's to the stitching line.*

PETAL PILLOW

Each of the petals of this pillow flower is a double layer, and the petals are sewn together in way that gives them even more dimension. The three-dimensional center of the flower is a clever embellishment that enhances the overall effect. Make several of these in different colors and start a garden in your living room!

PILLOW PARAMETERS

PILLOW TYPE: **Pillow Made with Pillow Form**

PILLOW TECHNIQUE:

Measure It: Pillow Dimension Guidelines . . . . . . p. 69

Pillow Forms and Other "Stuff" . . . . p. 67

🧵   **Making Fabric Flowers**

Fig. 3.27: *Petal Pillow.*

You'll Need:

Fabric:

• ³/₄ yard (68.5m) each, lightweight print and solid

Thread:

• All-purpose to match solid

• Monofilament

Miscellaneous:

- Ruler
- Hand needle (optional)
- Shears
- Pinking shears
- Clipping scissors
- Disappearing marker
- Hook-and-loop fastener
- 14" (35.5cm) pop-in round pillow form
- Tracing paper to make petal pattern

Pillow Progression

1. Place tracing paper over the petal pattern (found at the end of this chapter) and trace it. Cut 16 print and 16 solid petals. Place one print and one solid petal right sides together; stitch around all sides using a $^1/4$" (6mm) seam allowance. Repeat for 15 other petals.

   SEW-HOW: *Pink around each petal close to the seamline. This notches the seam allowance for smooth curves.*

2. Starting $1^1/2$" (4cm) from the point and on the solid side of each petal only, make a 3" (7.5cm) slit down center foldline one (Fig. 3.28). Turn petals right side out through this slit and press. The slit will be hidden inside the pillow cover.

3. Fold each petal on foldline two and press again (Fig. 3.29). Pin, then straight stitch petals together along foldline two (Fig. 3.30), matching print sides. Attach another petal as before, until you have completed the pillow front with eight petals stitched together in a circle.

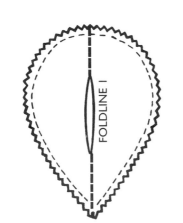

Fig. 3.28: *Make a 3" (7.5cm) slit down foldline one. Turn petals right side out and press.*

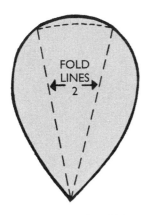

Fig. 3.29: *Fold each petal on foldline two and press again.*

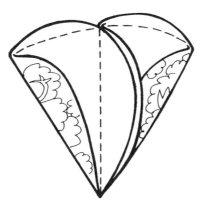

Fig. 3.30: *Pin, then straight stitch petals together along foldline two.*

4. Make the pillow back, this time making two four-petal halves. At the center of each half-circle, stitch hook-and-loop fastener on the top center on one half, and underneath the center on the other half. Stitch halves together, sewing in from the edge 2" (5cm) at foldline two on each side and leaving an opening for the pillow form.

5. To cover center points at the pillow front and back, prepare two flowers. Cut out several circles of print fabric in graduated sizes, beginning with a 2" (5cm) circle. Stack circles and set aside. Using the left-over print, cut several 1/2" × 5" (1.3cm × 12.5cm) bias strips; stack and stitch several of these and place on top of the circles (Fig. 3.31). Attach one flower to the center of front pillow cover. Knot strips individually and cut off excess fabric to create the center of the flower. Attach the second flower to the center of back pillow cover and finish the same way.

6. To stitch the pillow front and back together, use a ruler and disappearing marker and mark stitching lines across the top of each petal; place flowers, wrong sides together, then sew over marks using monofilament thread. Pop in the pillow and press the hook-and-loop fastener together to close or hand stitch the pillow opening, if you wish.

SEW HOW: *For more ideas using the slash-and-turn technique, refer to* Three-Dimensional Appliqué *by Jodie Davis (Chilton, 1993).*

Now that you've made a passel of playful pillows, try your hand at the romantic pillows and fantasy pillows in Chapter Four: Pillow Poetry and Fantasy.

A.

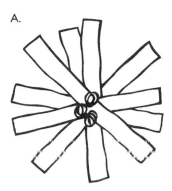

Fig. 3.31: *Cut several 1/2" × 5" (1.3cm × 12.5cm) strips on the bias. Stack and stitch several of these and place on top of the circles.*

B.

Chapter 3 Patterns

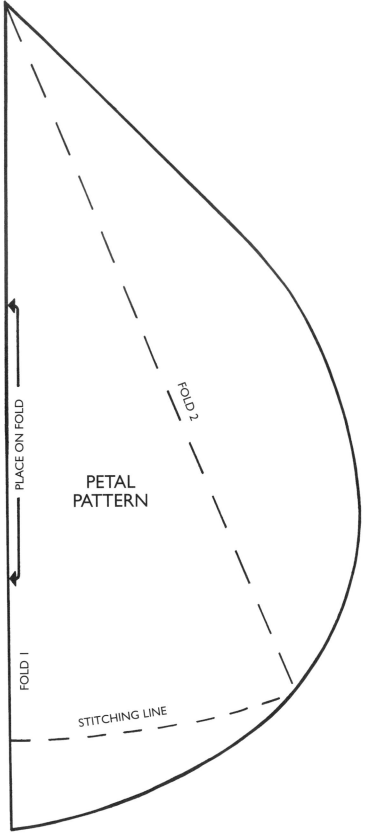

PLACE ON FOLD

FOLD 2

PETAL
PATTERN

FOLD 1

STITCHING LINE

Doodle Page

POSSIBLE PILLOW PROJECTS

Pillow I'd Like to Make	For What Room or Special Purpose?	Page #	Sketch of Pillow
1.			
2.			
3.			
4.			
5.			

Chapter 4

PILLOW POETRY AND FANTASY

Nine One-of-a-Kind Pillows to Keep or Give Away

In our quest to parley Pillows! Pillows! Pillows! into a parade of pillow pageantry, we've included this chapter called Pillow Poetry and Fantasy, which presents pillows not only as packages of palatial puffery, but pillows with a purpose (please…no punctilious pshaws) and a little fun (or should we say, phun?).

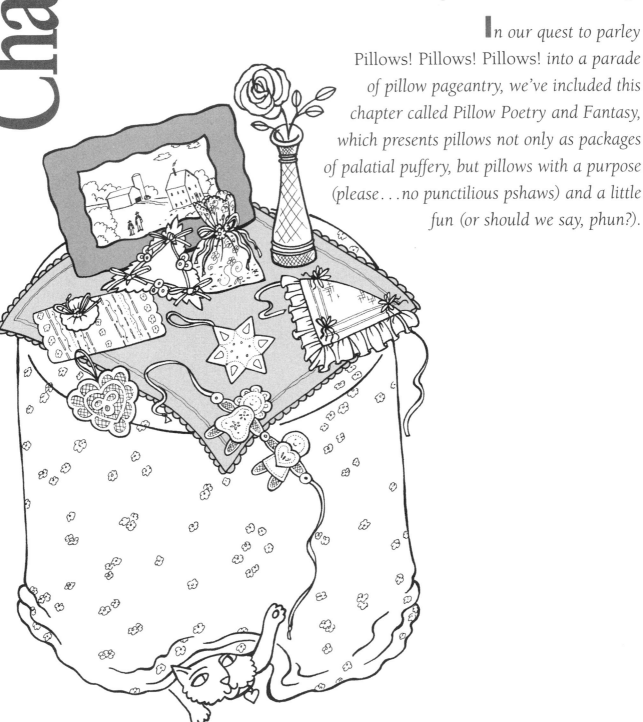

GINA'S SLEEP PILLOWS

Sleep pillows originated in Elizabethan times. These small packets of herbs, spices, and oils were slipped into bed pillows to induce sleep (different herbs brought different dreams). Included is a recipe from Gina Brown of Alberta, Canada — visit your library to find more. Find these and other herbs and potpourri at your local craft store.

Night Magic

- 1 cup rosemary
- 1 cup lemon verbena
- 2 cups pine needle

Crush very fine and blend all ingredients. For an instant refresher, sprinkle essential oil (available at crafts stores) in your favorite aromas on the pillow cover.

PILLOW PARAMETERS

PILLOW TYPE: **Pillow Stuffed with Herbs**

PILLOW TECHNIQUES:

 Making Potpourri Pillow Filler

 Decorating with Ribbons and Bows

 Decorating with Lace

 Envelop It: Making the Basic Envelope . . . . .p. 70

Lace or Battenburg Sleep Pillows
You'll Need:

Fabric:
- Two Battenburg or lace doilies
- Two or more Battenburg children (optional)
- Organdy the same size as the doilies

Thread:
- All-purpose to match fabric

Miscellaneous:
- Potpourri
- Ribbon roses (available at fabric and craft stores)

Pillow Progression

1. Combine two purchased Battenburg or lace doilies (found at fabric and craft stores). Back lace with organdy to keep the filling from sifting through.

2. Stitch around them with wrong sides together, and leaving an opening for the herbs. Stuff loosely; then close. Add ribbon roses to the corners.

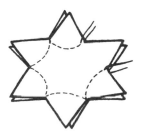

Fig. 4.1: *Lace or Battenburg Sleep Pillows.*

A.

VARIATIONS: *Stitch two Battenburg children together back-to-back, stuff with a little fiberfill, then close into a charming doll. Make two or more children, join their hands with* $1/4"$ *(6mm) wide satin ribbon and tie them across the top of a nursery mirror, use as a curtain tie back, or appliqué only one side of the doll to your pillow (Figs. 4.2a and 4.2b).*

Fig. 4.2: *Stitch Battenburg children back-to-back to make a doll, a pillow, or a charming decoration for a baby's room.*

B.

Fig. 4.3:
*Heirloom Hanky
Sleep Pillow.*

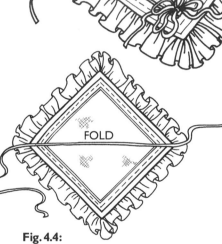

Fig. 4.4:
Fold decorative handkerchief into a triangle, slipping a narrow satin ribbon inside the fold.

Heirloom Hanky Sleep Pillow
You'll Need:
Fabric:
- One decorative handkerchief

Miscellaneous:
- Narrow satin ribbon
- Potpourri

Pillow Progression

1. Fold a decorative handkerchief into a triangle.

2. Slip a long, narrow satin ribbon inside the fold, extending it beyond the corners (for tying around the bedpost), as shown in Fig. 4.4.

3. Stitch edges part way closed, fill with herbs, then close the rest of the way.

Jackie's Wedding Dress Sleep Pillow
You'll Need:
Fabric:
- Scrap of embroidered organdy

Miscellaneous:
- Beads
- Potpourri
- Ribbons

Fig. 4.6: *Make a small bag of embroidered organdy, add beads, and tie closed with a ribbon.*

Fig. 4.5:
*Jackie's Wedding
Dress Sleep Pillow.*

Pillow Progression

1. Make a small bag of embroidered organdy (one with an embroidered edge works well). If it's fabric from a special event, all the better; this pillow was made from a scrap of Jackie's wedding dress (Fig. 4.6).

2. Fill with potpourri, then tie the bag closed at the top with ribbons, add beads, and hang on the mirror or bedpost.

Heirloom Sampler Sleep Pillow

You'll Need:

Fabric:

- Small squares of fabric
  (lace, embroidered insertion, and entredeau)
- Organdy the same size as the other fabric

Miscellaneous:

- Ribbon rose
- Bow

Pillow Progression

1. Make small squares of heirloom sewing using bits and pieces of lace, embroidered insertion, and entredeau (we used our heirloom samplers we made in a class).

2. Back sampler with a pastel organdy (Fig. 4.7).

3. Fold rectangle in an envelope shape and zigzag down each side. Fill, then close the back by hand (Fig. 4.8). Add a ribbon rose and a bow (available at specialty fabric and craft stores).

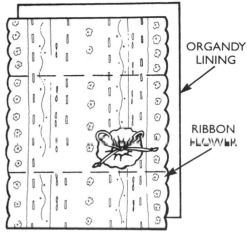

Fig. 4.7: *Heirloom Sampler Sleep Pillow. Back sampler with pastel organdy.*

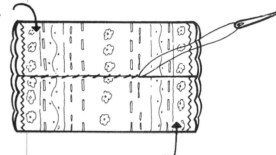

Fig. 4.8: *Fill, then close by hand. Add a ribbon rose and a bow.*

GRANDMOTHER'S FLOWER GARDEN PILLOW

Sometimes ideas grow out of necessity, as this one did. If you have shredded quilts that can no longer be used on a bed or as a wall-hanging, cut them into pillow shapes, add buttons, beads, ribbons, lace, and cover them with bridal tulle. Then add embroidery stitches to make your own heirloom.

Fig. 4.9: *Grandmother's Flower Garden Pillow.*

PILLOW PARAMETERS

PILLOW TYPE: **Pillow Made with Pillow Form**

PILLOW TECHNIQUES:

You'll Need:

Fabric:

- Damaged 14" (35.6cm) quilt square
- ½ yard (.45m) coordinating fabric for pillow back and ruffle
- Ruffle strip cut 5" × 4⅔ yards (13cm × 4.3m)
- Bridal tulle to cover front pillow square

Thread:

- Rayon, and cotton machine embroidery in colors to coordinate with quilt square
- All-purpose

Presser Feet:

- Darning
- Standard zigzag

Miscellaneous:

- Silky cord
- Buttons
- Beads
- Lace
- 14" (35.5cm) pillow form
- Various colors and types of ribbons

Pillow Progression

1. Find the damaged areas of your quilt square and begin arranging the decorations over the top.

2. Place and pin the tulle over the decorations that are over the quilt square to hold them in place. Tulle is magical and almost invisible. Following the design in the lace, freely embroider over the tulle, stitching around flower-shapes in the lace and couching over ribbons and appliqués (see Pillow Parameters Box).

3. Sew on buttons and beads after couching down the cords (serger braid can be used) and over the ribbons (Fig. 4.10; see Pillow Parameters Box).

4. Change to all-purpose thread top and bobbin and use the standard zigzag foot. Return the feed dogs to the up position. Make and apply the ruffle around the front pillow edge (see Pillow Parameters Box); then finish the pillow back, which is part of the envelope (Fig. 4.11; see Pillow Parameters Box).

VARIATIONS:

For more ideas, refer to Flower Garden Pillows in Jackie's book, Quick-Quilted Home Decor On Your Bernina *(Chilton, 1994).*

Fig. 4.10: *Sew on buttons and beads after couching down the cords and over the ribbons.*

Fig. 4.11: *Using a zigzag foot and all-purpose thread top and bobbin, make and apply the ruffle around the front of the pillow.*

WEDDING PILLOW

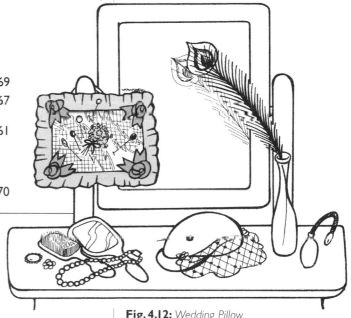

Fig. 4.12: *Wedding Pillow.*

You'll Need:

Fabric:

- Blue linen the same dimensions as piece of lace, enough for front and back plus seam allowances and overlap for the envelope closure

Thread:

- Monofilament
- All-purpose

Presser feet:

- Darning
- Standard zigzag

Miscellaneous:

- Piece of lace
- Hand needle
- Tear-away stabilizer
- Several fine silk pins
- Loose fiberfill
- Rotary cutter, mat, and ruler
- Prepleated ribbon twice the perimeter of the pillow (available at specialty heirloom stores and through mail order sources)
- 12" (30.5cm) length of ¼" (6mm) blue satin ribbon
- Four large ribbon roses or ribbon to make roses (available at craft and fabric stores)
- Four purchased blue silk buttons
- 24" (61cm) of ½" (1.3cm) ribbon

Note: The pillow size reflects the size of the lace so it necessitated our making an odd-shaped pillow form.

Pillow Progression

1. Back linen with tear-away stabilizer; then place lace on blue linen pillow top. Set your machine for free-machine embroidery and freely stitch the lace to the pillow top (see Pillow Parameters Box).

2. Stitch the pleated ribbon together into a loop. Then fold it in half at the seam, placing a pin at the opposite fold. Fold it in half again and mark with two more pins. Place the seam at the bottom front center of the pillow tops and center. Pull up the gathers with the gathering ribbon (included on the prepleated ribbon). Baste and stitch in place (Fig. 4.13). Machine or hand-tack a length of blue satin ribbon to pillow center to tie on the rings.

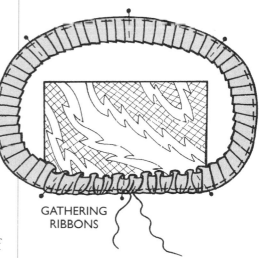

GATHERING RIBBONS

Fig. 4.13: *Place the seam at the bottom front center of the pillow tops and center. Pull up the gathers with the gathering string.*

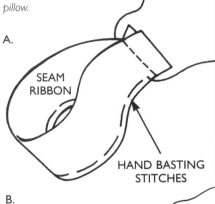

Fig.4.14: *To make a ribbon rose, seam the ribbon into a loop, hand baste along one edge of the loop, then pull on the basting stitches to gather the ribbon. Secure the thread ends and attach the rose to the pillow.*

A.

SEAM
RIBBON

HAND BASTING
STITCHES

B.

PULL BASTING
STITCHES INTO CIRCLE

3. Prepare the pillow back of the basic envelope (see Pillow Parameters Box). Sew or serge pillow front and back, right sides together.

4. Turn pillow case right side out. Hand stitch a large ribbon rose at each corner (Fig. 4.14). Stitch small blue silk buttons to the centers of the ribbon roses.

5. Since this is such a small, delicate pillow, fill it with small handfuls of loose fiberfill, then hand-stitch the envelope overlap closed in back.

VARIATIONS: *After the wedding, tie the center ribbon into a bow around a dried flower from the bride's bouquet or the groom's dried boutonniere; attach another long blue satin ribbon to the top corners at the pillow's underside, and tie the pillow onto the dresser mirror to hold stick pins, lapel pins, or other jewelry.*

PILLOW STORY STONES

Sometimes pillows are games. Each tiny pillow in this game is a story-stone with a design machine-stitched in the center. To play the game, each person pulls a story stone out of the bag, one by one. When the first is taken from the bag, the design on it begins the story. Then as others are pulled out, they enhance or move the plot along depending on the design on the story-stone pillow and the imagination of the story-teller. The story ends with the last stone.

Fig. 4.15:
Pillow Story Stones.

PILLOW PARAMETERS

PILLOW TYPE: **Pillow Quilted with Fusible Fleece**

PILLOW TECHNIQUE:

 Decorative Machine Stitching

You'll Need:

Fabric:

- Scraps of fabrics that don't ravel and in different colors (i.e., felt, faux leather or suede, polar fleece); if using one color fabric for the stones, you need a piece at least 45" × 15" (114cm × 38cm)

Presser Feet:

- Embroidery
- Blindhem/edgestitch

Thread:

- Machine embroidery in different colors
- Monofilament

Miscellaneous:
- Shears
- Ruler
- Chalk pencil
- Fusible fleece
- Seam sealant
- 2" (5cm) cardboard circle template

Pillow Progression

1. Fuse fleece on the wrong side of the felt following manufacturer's instructions. Mark the fabric into 2 ½" (6.5cm) squares with the chalk pencil, and ruler. Then mark a dot in the center of each square.

2. Thread your machine with one of the embroidery threads. Using your embroidery foot, test a few motifs in one square, checking for stitch uniformity and density. Stitch one motif in the center of each stone. If your machine has a stop, tie-off, or fix function, use it at the beginning and end of each motif, pull threads to the back of the fabric, dot with seam sealant; then cut threads ends off at the fabric.

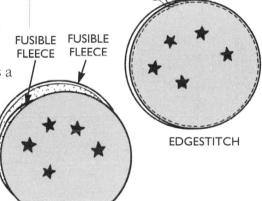

Fig. 4.16: *Cut out the stones into circle shapes.*

FUSIBLE FLEECE   FUSIBLE FLEECE

EDGESTITCH

3. Cut fabric into squares and place wrong sides together so there is a motif on each side of the stone. Center the 2" (5cm) circle template in the square and cut out the stones into circle shapes (Fig. 4.16). Rethread your machine with monofilament thread.

4. Stitch around the perimeter of the circles to finish the rest of the stones using the blindhem or edgestitch foot.

SEW-HOW: *You may have to lengthen the stitch slightly and reduce the foot pressure to compensate for the added thickness created by the fleece.*

VARIATIONS: *Use this as a travel game for children or adults. Rather than a general story, specify a mystery, or love story. Check the design possibilities on your machine. Use astrological signs for adults, dinosaurs for children, numbers, flowers, travel designs, sports motifs, or use an alphabet to spell out words.*

FUNNY FACES PILLOWS

Every child admitted to a local hospital in Chicago receives a dog or cat pillow with embroidered and appliquéd eyes, nose, tongue, and collar, which they take into surgery and take home afterward. The response of those hospitalized children? They love their comforting, comfortable pillows.

Our funny faces were inspired by those hospital pillows, but instead we made people-faces with interchangeable (and almost no-sew) features. The face can cry, laugh, look goofy, tired, studious, masculine, feminine — even like

Fig. 4.17: *Funny Faces Pillows.*

a clown. The funny features, hair, beards, mustaches, and bow ties are backed with the hook side of the hook-and-loop fastener, which adheres to the felt without the use of the other side. We used sticky-back felt so almost anyone can make these funny features — just trace, cut, peel, and stick.

PILLOW PARAMETERS

PILLOW TYPE: **Pillow Made with Pillow Form**

PILLOW TECHNIQUES:

You'll Need:

Fabric:

- One 13" (33cm) flesh-colored circle and one 13" (33cm) brown circle of good quality felt
- Felt scraps in assorted colors; 9" × 12" (23cm × 33.5cm) Sticky-back felt in assorted colors (we used Kunin Presto-Felt with good results)
- Four to five 9" × 12" (23cm × 30.5cm) felt pieces to make a book to hold the funny features

Thread:

- Monofilament

Miscellaneous:

- Buttons
- Ribbons
- Hand needle
- Pencil or fabric marker
- Shears and trimming scissors
- 12" (30.5cm) round pop-in pillow form
- Tracing paper
- Rickrack to create hair
- Hook-and-loop fastener tape
- All-purpose thread and thimble

Pillow Progression

1. Place felt circles right sides together. Machine-stitch around the circle using a ½" (1.3cm) seam allowance and leaving an opening large enough for the pillow form to fit through and for turning. Turn felt pillow cover right sides out, pop in the pillow form and close the opening by hand.

2. Trace the funny feature patterns at the end of this chapter onto tracing paper. Cut one plain felt rectangle for the back of each funny feature, slightly larger than needed. It will be trimmed to size later.

3. Thread your machine and sew the hook-side strip (of hook-and-loop fastener) to the wrong side of the plain felt rectangle.

4. To make "The Big Mouth," trace and cut out the tongue, teeth, and lips from the sticky-back felt, leaving the paper on each piece.

5. To assemble the mouth, place the plain felt rectangle back, hook-side down on a table. Peel off the paper from the back of the tongue and position it on the rectangle, sticky side down and with hook-side tape centered on the feature. Next, peel and stick on the teeth. Finally, peel and stick on the lips. Trim excess felt so edges are even — voilà: "The Big Mouth."

6. Repeat steps four and five to create the rest of the features, remembering to work from the base and stack each element on top of the previous one.

7. To keep the funny features in place, stack four or five 9" × 12" (23cm × 30.5cm) plain felt squares, aligning all edges. Stitch along one long edge using a 1/2" (1.3cm) seam allowance to create a book. Store the funny features in the pages of the book.

VARIATIONS: To convert a regular round pillow to a funny face pillow, make The Pop-in Pillow Cover (see Chapter Two) in different felt colors for more people and animal choices. If the funny features book gets too full, make a separate book for noses, eyes, hair, etc., and if your sewing machine writes, customize the books for each child's funny features (i.e. Jennifer's Funny Noses, Julie's Funny Ears, or Todd's Funny Hair).

OTHER PILLOW FANTASY IDEAS

- Take handles off a flat tote bag. Fill and sew or fuse up the opening. Add tassels to the corners.
- Hand baste or use a pressure sensitive adhesive (look for Sticky Stuff or Insta Tack) to apply collectible embroidered pieces to the front of a ready-made pillow.
- Use your child's kindergarten drawing of him or herself as a pattern to make a bed doll, a flat quilt-like outline of themselves. Cut out front and back pieces, fill with batting; then paint and dress the bed doll using fabric from his or her clothing or from a favorite piece of outgrown clothing.
- How tall is your child? Add another 12" (30.5cm) and make a rectangular floor pillow using this measurement as the pillow's width. Stuff the pillow lightly with fiberfill.
- Use our ideas in miniature and make bean bags or pin cushions.

We hope the previous "what-to-do" chapters have been inspirational. Now take a look at our "how-to-do-it" Pillow Primer in "Way Past Plain: Professional Pointers for Producing Pillow Personality," next in Chapter Five.

Fig. 4.18:
Other Pillow Fantasy Ideas.

Chapter 4 Patterns

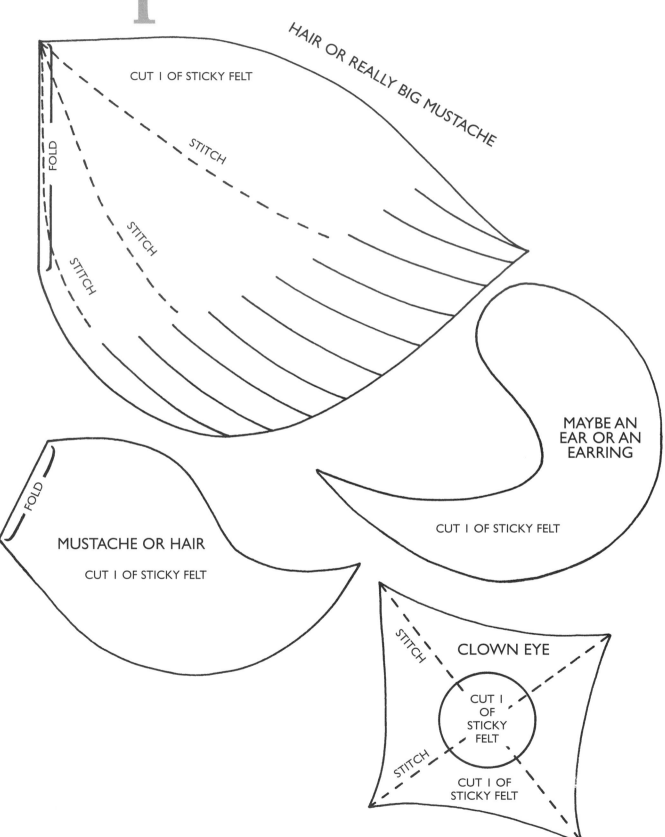

HAIR OR REALLY BIG MUSTACHE

CUT 1 OF STICKY FELT

FOLD

STITCH

STITCH

STITCH

MAYBE AN
EAR OR AN
EARRING

CUT 1 OF STICKY FELT

FOLD

MUSTACHE OR HAIR

CUT 1 OF STICKY FELT

CLOWN EYE

STITCH

STITCH

CUT 1
OF
STICKY
FELT

CUT 1 OF
STICKY FELT

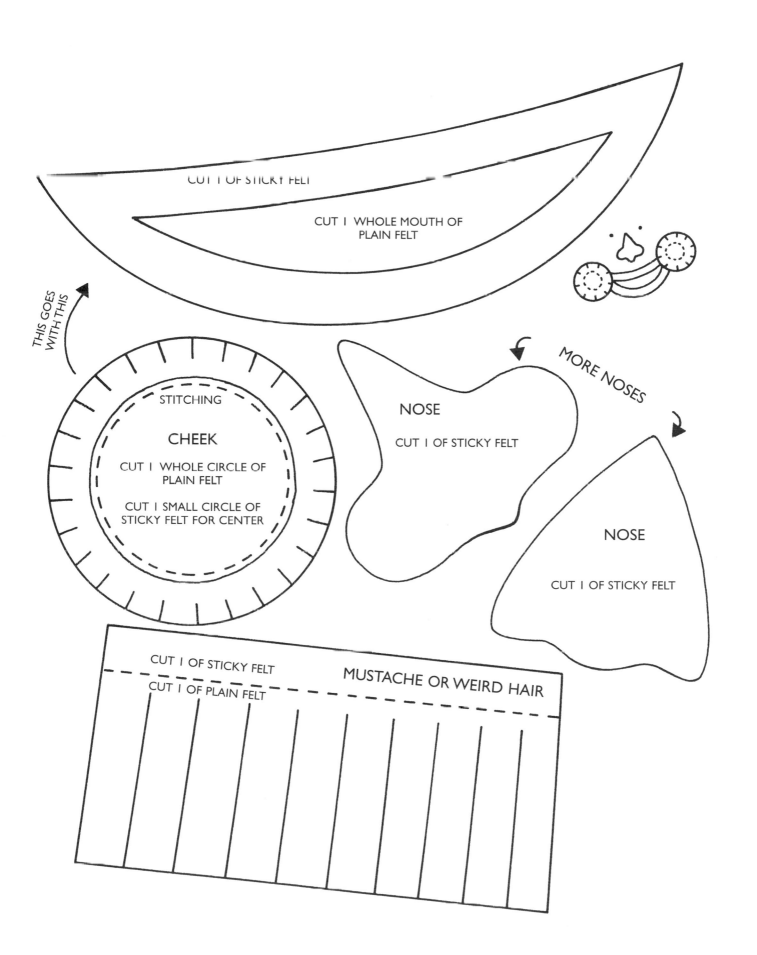

CUT 1 OF STICKY FELT

CUT 1 WHOLE MOUTH OF
PLAIN FELT

THIS GOES
WITH THIS

STITCHING

CHEEK

CUT 1 WHOLE CIRCLE OF
PLAIN FELT

CUT 1 SMALL CIRCLE OF
STICKY FELT FOR CENTER

NOSE

CUT 1 OF STICKY FELT

MORE NOSES

NOSE

CUT 1 OF STICKY FELT

CUT 1 OF STICKY FELT

CUT 1 OF PLAIN FELT

MUSTACHE OR WEIRD HAIR

Chapter 4 Patterns

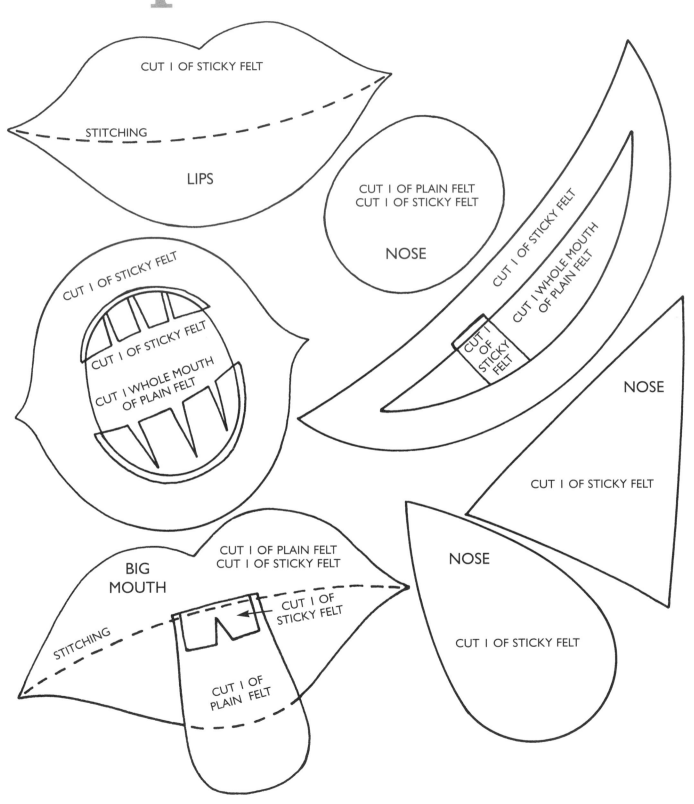

CUT 1 OF STICKY FELT

STITCHING

LIPS

CUT 1 OF PLAIN FELT
CUT 1 OF STICKY FELT

NOSE

CUT 1 OF STICKY FELT

CUT 1 OF STICKY FELT

CUT 1 WHOLE MOUTH
OF PLAIN FELT

CUT 1 OF STICKY FELT

CUT 1 WHOLE MOUTH
OF PLAIN FELT

CUT 1 OF STICKY FELT

NOSE

CUT 1 OF STICKY FELT

BIG
MOUTH

CUT 1 OF PLAIN FELT
CUT 1 OF STICKY FELT

CUT 1 OF
STICKY FELT

STITCHING

NOSE

CUT 1 OF STICKY FELT

CUT 1 OF
PLAIN FELT

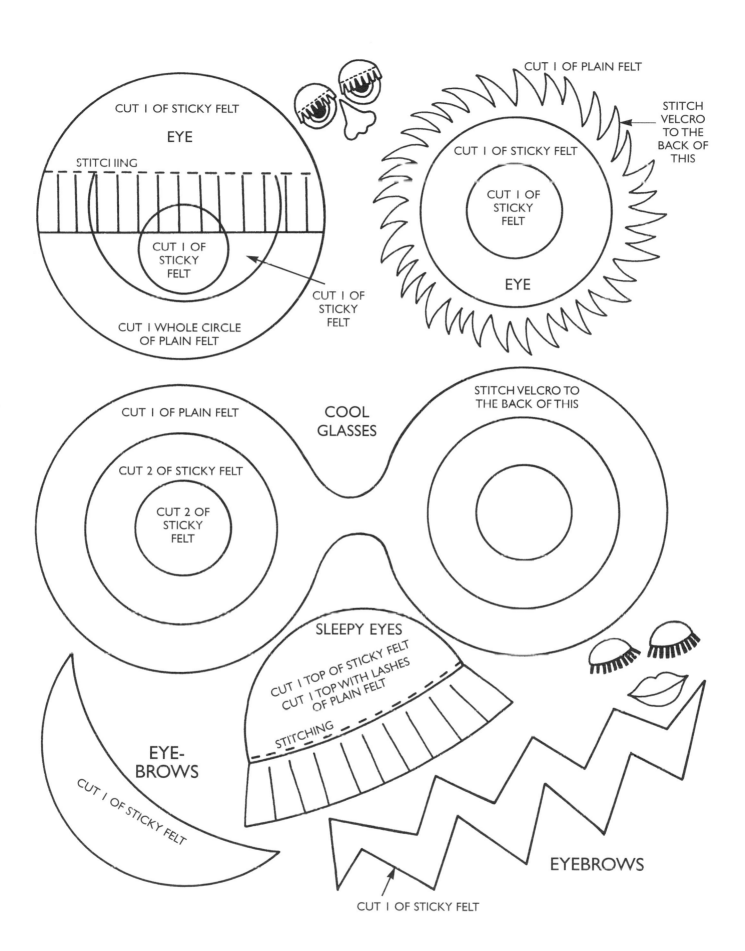

CUT 1 OF STICKY FELT

EYE

STITCHING

CUT 1 OF STICKY FELT

CUT 1 OF STICKY FELT

CUT 1 WHOLE CIRCLE OF PLAIN FELT

CUT 1 OF PLAIN FELT

STITCH VELCRO TO THE BACK OF THIS

CUT 1 OF STICKY FELT

CUT 1 OF STICKY FELT

EYE

CUT 1 OF PLAIN FELT

CUT 2 OF STICKY FELT

CUT 2 OF STICKY FELT

COOL GLASSES

STITCH VELCRO TO THE BACK OF THIS

EYE-BROWS

CUT 1 OF STICKY FELT

SLEEPY EYES

CUT 1 TOP OF STICKY FELT
CUT 1 TOP WITH LASHES OF PLAIN FELT

STITCHING

EYEBROWS

CUT 1 OF STICKY FELT

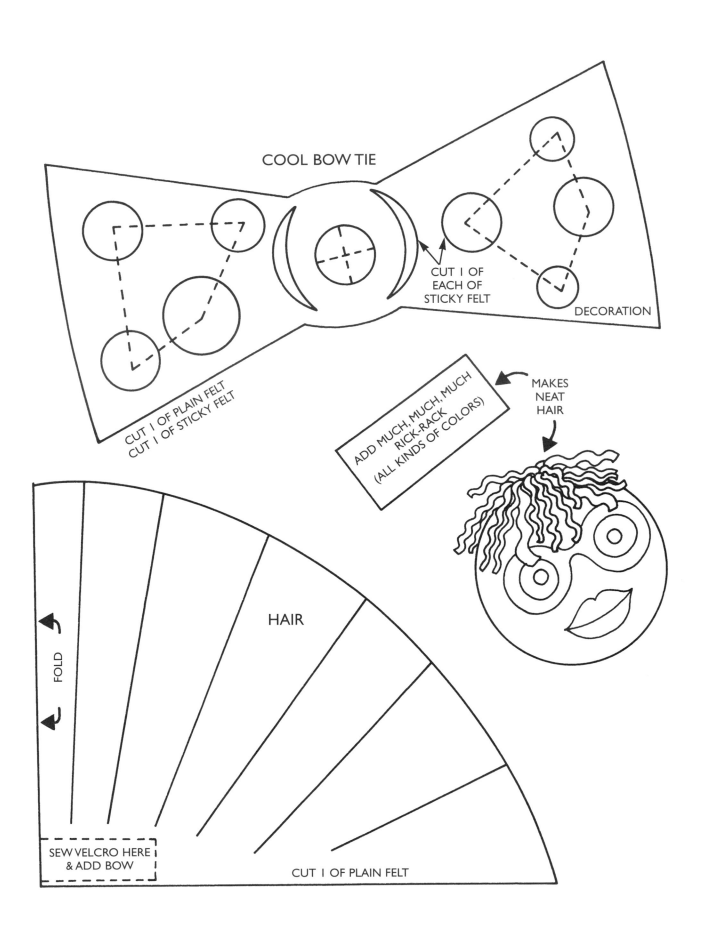

COOL BOW TIE

CUT 1 OF
EACH OF
STICKY FELT

DECORATION

CUT 1 OF PLAIN FELT
CUT 1 OF STICKY FELT

ADD MUCH, MUCH, MUCH
RICK-RACK
(ALL KINDS OF COLORS)

MAKES
NEAT
HAIR

HAIR

FOLD

SEW VELCRO HERE
& ADD BOW

CUT 1 OF PLAIN FELT

Doodle Page

POSSIBLE PILLOW PROJECTS

Pillow I'd Like to Make	For What Room or Special Purpose?	Page #	Sketch of Pillow
1.			
2.			
3.			
4.			
5.			

Chapter 5

WAY PAST PLAIN

Professional Pointers for Producing Pillow Personality

We've presented projects aplenty in this book, and we hope that by now you've tried a few. But we also want you to be inspired to create your own original pillow designs. In this chapter we provide the lowdown on decorating pillows, from enhancing pre-made pretties using decorator trims, tapes, and tassels to creating distinctive edges (with gathers and ruffles) and sensational pillow surfaces (using our easy embellishment techniques). Why settle for plain pillows when pillow pizazz and personality are literally at your fingertips?

DECORATOR TRIMS: BRAID, CORD, WELTING, FRINGE, AND TASSELS

Decorator trims, available through local fabric and home decorating stores, can be used separately or together to add color and pizzazz to any home decorating project. When we visited the decorator-trim departments in our local fabric stores, the choices were almost daunting, so I asked Victoria Waller, Home Decorating Product Manager for Prym-Dritz, to give us a glossary of trim terms and her favorite insertion tips. She recommends coordinating trim colors using your fabric as a color guide, then layering trims of associated colors to add depth and interest.

The basic types of decorator trims are: braid, cord, welting (also known as piping), fringe, and tassels. After giving you Victoria's basic instructions for attaching trim, we list each category of trim, any variations within that category of trim (Mandarin braid, for example), and Victoria's tips for attaching the trim.

The Basics of Attaching Trim

Although Victoria generally recommends sewing trims on with a large multi-purpose or universal sewing machine needle, she points out that "many of the new glues, fusibles, or press-on adhesives make beautiful pillows that are no-sew, too. . .just remember to check that the adhesives, like the trims, are Dry-Clean Only." For more information on how to decorate pillows and other home decorating projects with decorator trims, look for how-to booklets where decorator trims are sold. Also see "Decorate It" in Chapter 6.

Victoria's Overall Tips for Attaching Trim

- Use a size 14/90-16/100 universal or sharp needle in both the sewing machine and serger.
- Use a long 3-4mm (six to eight stitches per inch) stitch length when attaching trims and sewing through multiple thicknesses.
- Stitch slowly over thick areas to prevent needle breakage.
- Use a zipper or piping foot for most applications.
- Start trim at the center of any side unless the pillow design dictates not to.
- Fabric and trim length must be of equal lengths — never pull the trim to fit.
- Most fringe has a row of protective chainstitching along the cut edge; remove it *after* insertion.
- Sew trim to front pillow piece, right sides together, then attach pillow back.

Braid Types

Braid is a flat trim with two finished edges.

Gimp is a flat braid usually used to conceal upholstery tacks. Use it also for decorating boxes and to accent borders, and as a way to conceal or embellish a color-blocked seam.

Fig. 5.1: *Braid is a flat trim with two finished edges that can be attached by gluing, fusing, or sewing.*

UPHOLSTERY

Glue

BRAID

BUTT EDGE   TAPE END

TWISTED POLYESTER CABLE CORD

Fig.5.2: *Twisted polyester cable cord.*

TAPE AND CUT

Fig.5.3: *Place a strip of tape around the cord before cutting through it to prevent uncontrolled fraying.*

CHAIR TIE

Fig.5.4: *Use chair ties as curtain tie backs or cut them apart to use in home decorating projects.*

Mandarin braid is a ¹/₂" (1.3cm) dimensional gimp that is great for outlining place mats, pillows, and other home decorating projects, as well as craft items such as boxes and lamp shades. It makes a terrific fashion accent on vests, hats, and accessories too.

Attaching Braid

Glue, fuse, or straight-stitch braid over a join, being careful that both edges are secure. If fusing, note the fiber content and do not use a too-hot iron unless the braid is protected by a press cloth (Fig. 5.1).

Cord Types

Cord is a round, twisted edging and comes in widths from ¹/₈" to ¹/₂" (3mm - 1.3cm). Cord can be a shiny rayon, spun satiny rayon, cotton, or combined fibers (e.g., rayon and cotton), each creating a unique texture. Stitch cord to pillows, table coverings, or almost any home decorating project.

Cable cord is a twisted cotton or polyester cord used for making your own piping or welting and used to trim pillows, slip covers, and for fashion sewing projects (Fig. 5.2). To cut cable cord, tape it, then cut through the tape so ends won't fray out (Fig. 5.3). If the cord is 100% cotton, wrap it around your hand, pull the hank of cord off your hand and put a rubber band around the center of it, pre-shrink the cord in hot water, and dry it in a dryer. For tips on attaching welting, see "Attaching Welting Made From Cable Cord" later in this chapter.

Chair tie is a cord 27" - 30" (68.5cm - 76cm) long with tassels on both ends. Traditionally used to attach cushions to chairs, it may be used as well for curtain tie-backs. Or cut it apart for other home decorating, craft, and fashion sewing projects (Fig. 5.4).

Cord-edge is a decorator twisted cord with a "lip edge" on one side. The "lip" or "gimp" edge makes it easy to insert between a seam in a pillow, or at the edge of a cornice, swag, or jabot (see Figs. 5.7 - 5.10). Widths vary from ³/₁₆" to ¹/₂" (5mm - 1.3cm).

Filler cord is a web-covered cotton cord used inside piping and/or welt edging. Softer than twisted cable cord, filler cord is often used to make shirred piping, too (Fig. 5.5). Filler cord is available from ⁵/₃₂" to 1³/₄" (5mm - 4.5cm). Pre-shrinking is not recommended, so be sure to "Dry-Clean Only" all filler-cord projects.

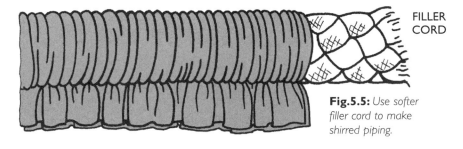

FILLER CORD

Fig.5.5: *Use softer filler cord to make shirred piping.*

Attaching Cord or Chair Tie

Using monofilament thread or thread that matches the cord, attach the cord by hand or use the piping or cording foot on your sewing machine to couch down cord with a zigzag.

Attaching Cord-Edge

1. Start anywhere but a corner, and be sure to leave a tail of more than 3" (7.5cm) of cord at your starting point.

2. When you come to a corner, clip the lip to the cord and nudge the cord to form some ease by pushing your finger into the corner (Fig. 5.6). This will create clean-looking corners.

3. When you reach your starting point, overlap the two pieces of cord (Fig. 5.7). Cut the cords so that they have 3" (7.5cm) tails. You are now ready to create an invisible join.

   SEW HOW: *Remember to place a strip of tape around the cord before cutting through it to prevent uncontrolled fraying (see Fig. 5.3).*

4. On the tails only, clip the chainstitch that joins the cord to the gimp (Fig. 5.8).

5. Starting at the overlap, pull gimp away from the cord, untwisting the cord tail (Fig. 5.9).

6. Overlap the twists at the join, so the cord plies line up and the cut ends extend into the seam allowance (Fig. 5.10).

7. Stitch over the tails so the ends are in the seam allowance.

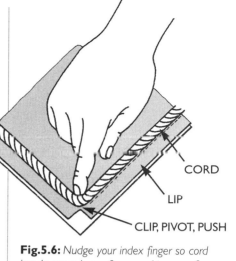

Fig.5.6: *Nudge your index finger so cord bends around your finger and is away from the needle.*

CORD

LIP

CLIP, PIVOT, PUSH

Fig.5.7: *When attaching cord edge, start and stop by overlapping the cord ends.*

Fig.5.8: *On the tails only, clip the chainstitch that joins the cord to the gimp.*

Fig.5.9: *Pin cord ends in place over lip. (A piece of tape helps keep the untwisted cords in place.)*

Fig.5.10: *Overlap twists so cord plies line up and the cut ends extend into the seam allowance.*

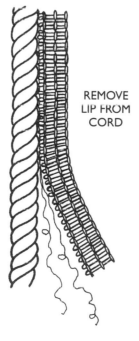

"LIP" OR GIMP EDGE

OVERLAP AND TAPER NARROW WIDTHS

REMOVE LIP FROM CORD

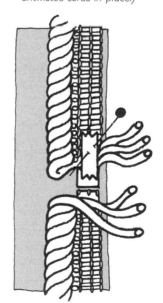

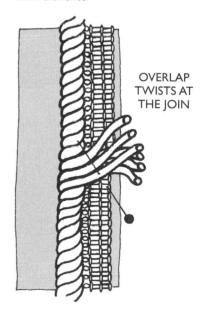

OVERLAP TWISTS AT THE JOIN

Welting, or Piping

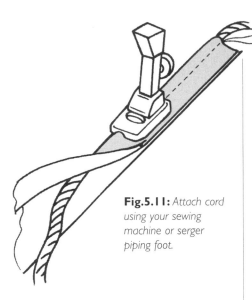

Welting, also referred to as piping, is cable or filler cord covered with straight- or bias-cut fabric. It has a ¹/₄" (6mm) seam allowance for easy insertion. If the fabric is cut on the cross or lengthwise grain, it can be used on square slip covers and pillows, but it will not shape smoothly around curves (unless it is shirred onto the filler cord).

If the fabric is cut on the bias, the welting/piping will shape smoothly around curves such as round pillows. Piping reinforces seams, in addition to giving a clean, tailored look to both home decorating and fashion sewing projects.

Fig.5.11: *Attach cord using your sewing machine or serger piping foot.*

Attaching Welting Made from Cable Cord

1. To cover cable cord with fabric, seam bias-cut fabric strips cut the circumference of the cord plus ¹/₂" (1.3cm) for ¹/₄" (6mm) seam allowances. For thicker cord add 1" (2.5cm) for ¹/₂" (1.3cm) seam allowances.

   SEW-HOW: Although fabric-covered cord is available by the yard and may be found in the home decorator trim area of your local fabric store, the piping you make and cover yourself can be cut across the grain to save on fabric.

2. Attach the covered cord to the right side of your pillow top by using the piping or zipper foot on your sewing machine or serger (Fig. 5.11).

3. Clip piping seam allowance to the stitching at each corner, without cutting through the cord (Fig. 5.12). With the needle in the fabric, raise the foot and pivot. Nudge your index finger into the corner so the cord bends around your finger and is away from the needle (see Fig. 5.6). Lower the presser foot and stitch.

4. Place your pillow top and back right sides together so the stitching from the previous step is where you can see it.

5. Decenter the needle on your sewing machine so that it falls between the previous row of stitching and the bump of the piping. This way, you're sewing close enough to the cord that you won't see the previous row of stitching when the pillow is turned right side out.

6. Butt cord ends at the join. Tape the cord ends together. Turn fabric edge under and place it so it overlaps the other side (Fig. 5.13). Stitch the join.

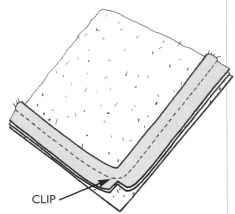

CLIP

Fig.5.12: *Clip the corners, being careful not to cut into the cord.*

Fig.5.13: *Open piping on one side, cut cord, and butt the ends (a). When covering a cable cord join, butt cord ends, turn fabric under, and release a few stitches on the other side (b). Overlap the fabric, then stitch the join (c).*

A.

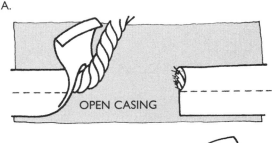

OPEN CASING

B.

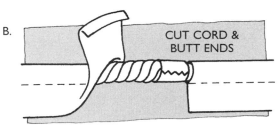

CUT CORD & BUTT ENDS

C.

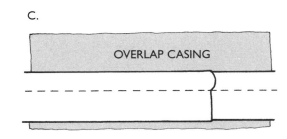

OVERLAP CASING

Anatomy of a Decorator Fringe

Fringe is a decorative edging consisting of hanging packed yarns, permanently looped and stitched on one side and looped or cut on the opposite side.

Chainstitch is the looped row of stitching used at the cut edge of the fringe to prevent tangling when sewing (Fig. 5.14a). It is also used to connect the gimp to the cord in a cord-edge. The chainstitch is designed for easy removal, just pull the thread end to remove it *after* installing fringe in your pillow or home decorating project.

Header edge is the top, looped, and stitched edge of the fringe, which is usually inserted into the seam allowance (Fig. 5.14b).

Gimp edge is the flat edge attached to the cord edge and tassel-fringe (Fig. 5.14c). Insert the gimp edge into a seam allowance or use decoratively on the outside of the project.

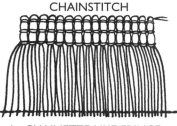
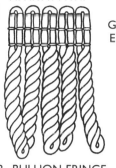

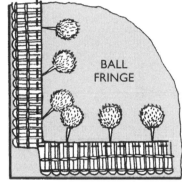

CHAINSTITCH

A. CHAINETTE-LIKE FRINGE

HEADER EDGE

GIMPE EDGE

B. BULLION FRINGE

C. TASSEL FRINGE

Fig.5.14: *Header edge and gimp edge are at the top of fringe for in-seam application. The chainstitch keeps fringe from tangling and is removed after application.*

Fringe Types

Ball fringe is a decorative edging constructed of fluffy cotton balls. It's great for whimsical decorating, children's decor, and costume sewing (Fig. 5.15).

Bouclé fringe is a fringe constructed of nubby, permanently kinked yarn. Bouclé fringe can be long, short, looped, or bullion.

Bullion fringe is a long fringe with twisted, looped ends — perfect for upholstery, slipcovers, table covers, pillows, and window treatments — it even makes great doll hair (see Fig. 5.14b).

Brush or moss fringe is a short cut fringe which creates a full brush effect when sewn into a project such as pillows, upholstery, slip covers, and window treatments. Do not remove the chainstitch that holds the free ends of the fringe together until *after* it has been attached (Fig. 5.16a). When attaching brush or moss fringe, attach the fringe header to the pillow top flat or as an in-seam insertion. Butt the fringe ends together at the join (5.16b). Never overlap because two rows of fringe create uneven fluff and bulk.

Butterfly fringe is a fringe with cut edges on two sides connected by an open threaded area. When stitched and folded in half the long way, it creates a double-thick row of fringe.

Chainette fringe is a fringe constructed of many chainette ends (see Fig. 5.14a). It is commonly called "flapper fringe." Short or long, it's great for window treatments, table covers, and fashion sewing.

Tassel fringe is a trim consisting of tiny tassels attached to a row of gimp with chainette cord. Add tassel fringe to almost any home decorating project for depth and surface interest (see Fig. 5.14c).

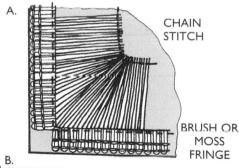

BALL FRINGE

Fig.5.15: *When attaching fringe, clip through gimp header at each corner.*

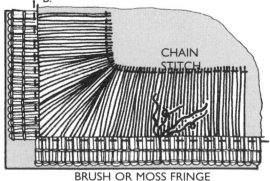

A.

CHAIN STITCH

BRUSH OR MOSS FRINGE

B.

CHAIN STITCH

BRUSH OR MOSS FRINGE

Fig.5.16: *Butt the fringe ends together at the join on moss or brush fringe.*

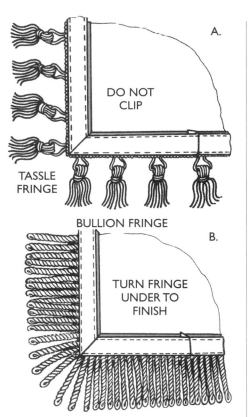

TASSLE FRINGE

DO NOT CLIP

BULLION FRINGE

TURN FRINGE UNDER TO FINISH

Fig. 5.17: *Miter corners and stitch both sides to apply tassel, bullion, or flat fringe.*

Attaching Fringe

1. Most fringes can be attached flat to the base fabric by sewing through both sides of the header or by fusing, then stitching it on (Fig. 5.17a). Miter the corners for a clean, professional finish (Fig. 5.17b).

2. For a seam insertion, stitch the header flush to the pillow front edge using a ¹/₂" (1.3cm) seam allowance, so that the fringe, tassels, or balls show on the right side (see Fig. 5.15). Clip through gimp or header at each corner. For all fringe except brush/moss fringe, butt thick fringe or overlap thin ones turning ends under to finish.

Tassels

Tassels are made of thread strands tied or banded at the top. Tassels are available with either a ¹/₂" (1.3cm) or 3" (7.5cm) long top loop for easy attachment. Use them to trim pillows, table toppers, and window shades, or make drapery tie backs, jewelry, and other home decorating projects.

Attaching Tassels

1. Hand-stitch tassels with small loops. To reinforce the loop, add a drop of glue or seam sealant to the knot in the thread, pass the needle and thread through the tassel, and snug the knot up and inside the tassel (Fig. 5.18).

2. To attach tassels with long loops to pillow corners, position tassel head ¹/₂" (1.3cm) outside the seamline so the tassel loop is inside the seam allowance (Fig. 5.19a). Machine stitch, pulling the loop for a snug fit as you go (Fig. 5.19b).

Fig. 5.18: *Hand stitch tassels with small loops, then add a drop of liquid seam sealant where tassel is attached.*

FOR SHORT LOOP ATTACH BY HAND

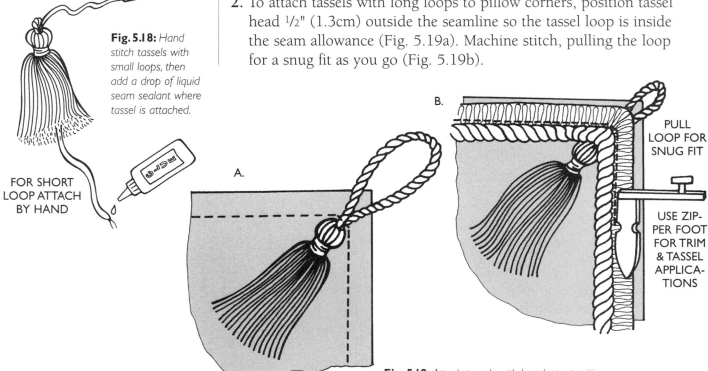

PULL LOOP FOR SNUG FIT

USE ZIPPER FOOT FOR TRIM & TASSEL APPLICATIONS

Fig. 5.19: *Attach tassels with long loops, positioning them ¹/₂" (1.3cm) from the corner (a). Pull the loop for a snug fit (b).*

GATHERS AND RUFFLES FOR GREAT-LOOKING EDGES

Gathers and ruffles add dimension and interest to pillows and other home dec projects. What follows are the products and techniques that make gathering fast, easy, and professional-looking.

Decorator and Shirring Tapes: No-Sew and Easy-To-Sew Options

Although decorator tapes are generally thought of in connection with making draperies, several types can be used for smaller pillow projects. *Sew-on tapes* can be used by stitching between the cords and shirring up a ruffle or gathering a strip and creating a textured surface design (Fig. 5.20). Gosling is the best-selling brand.

Iron-on decorator tapes are fused — rather than sewn — onto a project. The most widely distributed tapes are from Dritz, although Conso and Mastex iron-on tapes are also available (Fig. 5.21). Janis Bullis, a designer for Prym-Dritz Corporation, uses iron-on shirring tapes to create surface designs (Fig. 5.22). See her pillow (submitted by Dianne Giancola) in the color pages and in the Designer Showcase Key.

> **SEW-HOW:** *To make detachable ruching, pull in shirring cords, then wrap and knot them into a figure eight around a small piece of cardboard, tucking the cardboard under the ruched strip. That way the fullness can be let out and pressed flat after laundering.*

For more uses for decorator tapes, read *Gail Brown's All-New Instant Interiors* (Open Chain Publishing/Chilton, 1992).

Elastic shirring tape (available through your local fabric store or favorite mail-order source) is an easy-to-use elastic treatment for creating dimension on pillows and for fashion sewing projects. Look for Stitch 'n Stretch elastic treatment. Cut treatment the same length as the flat length or circumference plus seam allowances. Pull out spandex cords 1/2" (1.3cm) from each end of the woven band. If this is being applied in the round, fold under the short ends of the woven band. Pin and stitch it on flat, guiding along the marked lines. Pull elastic cords out at each end as needed and tie them off (Fig. 5.23). *Don't cut the cords.* As with the decorator shirring tapes, pull in elastic cords, wrap cords in a figure eight around cardboard, and tuck the wrapped cardboard into the pillow. Release the cords for laundering and pressing, and pull them up again around the pillow.

Easy Filler-Cord Gathering

Rather than running two rows of machine basting stitches and pulling up the gathers, zigzag or serge over a filler cord such as dental floss, fishing line, or crochet cotton. When you pull up the gathers, the stress is on the filler cord so gathering is even and gathering threads won't break.

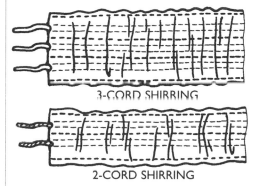

Fig. 5.20: *Use sew-on tapes for a removable pillow ruching.*

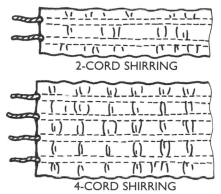

Fig. 5.21: *Two-cord and four-cord shirring iron-on-tape.*

Fig. 5.22: *No-Sew Ruffle Pillow using iron-on shirring tapes.*

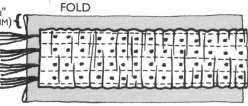

Fig. 5.23: *Cinch in a pillow slipcover using Stitch 'n Stretch elastic treatment. Sew along the marked lines, pull in the cords as needed and tie them off.*

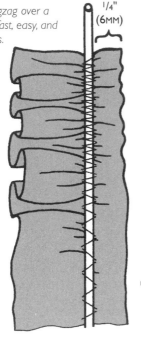

SEAM ALLOWANCE

¹/₄" (6mm)

Fig. 5.24: *Zigzag over a filler cord for fast, easy, and secure gathers.*

Filler-Cord Gathering on Your Sewing Machine

1. Using all-purpose thread top and bobbin, set your sewing machine for a 2.5 width, two-length (12 stitches per inch) zigzag.

2. Lay the filler cord (floss or crochet cotton) just inside the seamline and under your embroidery foot. Sew, being careful not to stitch through the cord (Fig. 5.24). Pull up gathers the desired length.

   SEW-HOW: *Some embroidery and accessory feet have holes or guides to guide cord for this and other couching techniques. Check your Operating Manual or refer to* Teach Yourself To Sew Better — A Step-By-Step Guide To Your Sewing Machine *by Jan Saunders (Chilton, 1990).*

Filler-Cord Gathering on Your Serger

1. Set your serger for a wide, medium-length, balanced three-thread stitch.

2. Guide the filler cord over the toe of the foot, between the needle and knives, and then under the back of the foot. Serge.

   SERGING SAVVY: *Your serger may have a cording guide in the standard foot or a piping foot available that will keep the filler cord straight and prevent the knives from cutting off the filler cord. Check your feet and look in your Operating Manual (Fig. 5.25).*

3. Serge over the filler cord for about 2" (5cm), stop, lift the presser foot, then place the edge of the fabric under the foot and continue to serge over the cord (see Fig. 5.25).

4. At the end of the fabric, lift the presser foot and move the cord out of the way of the stitches and chain off. Anchor the beginning of the cord with a pin and a figure eight, then pull up the gathers as needed (Fig. 5.26).

5. Attach the filler-cord gathered ruffle to the pillow top, stitching just to the left of the filler cord gathers (Fig. 5.27).

Fig. 5.25:

Guide filler cord under the back of the foot and between the knives and the front of the foot (or use the guide in your standard foot). Serge over about 2" (5cm) of cord, lift the presser foot, then place the edge of the fabric under the foot and continue to serge over the cord.

Fig. 5.26:

At the end, lift the foot and move the cord out of the way. Chain off.

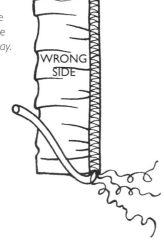

WRONG SIDE

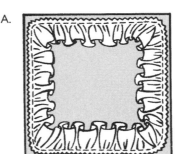

A.

B.

Fig. 5.27: *Pull up gathers and seam ruffle ends. Attach ruffle to pillow top, stitching just under the filler cord gathers.*

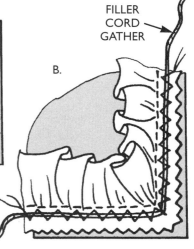

FILLER CORD GATHER

56 *Pillows! Pillows! Pillows!*

Easier Gathering Using Machine Accessories

If you don't need your gathers to be adjustable, then you may want to use your gathering foot or shirring attachment, both of which are available for your sewing machine or serger.

Using the Gathering Foot on Your Sewing Machine

The gathering foot (usually *not* a standard accessory foot) gathers light- to medium-weight fabric automatically. It's great for sewing ruffles and making puffing strips. The underside is raised behind the needle, and the slot in front of the needle enables you to gather and attach a ruffle simultaneously. To use the gathering foot:

1. Set your machine for a straight stitch. The amount the fabric gathers is determined by the weight of the fabric, the stitch length, and upper thread tension. Use a fine fabric, a long stitch, and a tighter tension for a lot of gathers.

   SEW-HOW: *To determine how much fabric will gather, cut a strip of fabric 10" (25.5cm) long, and prepare it as though you intend to use it for the finished ruffle (as described in step two). Sew or serge the ruffle until you get the desired look, then measure the gathered edge. If 10" (25.5cm) gathers down to 5" (12.5cm), then you'll use a two to one ratio.*

2. To gather and attach a ruffle onto a flat piece of fabric, place the fabric to be gathered under the foot, right side up; then lower the presser foot. Slip the flat piece that will attach to the ruffle into the slot, right side down; then stitch. A far left needle position will give you more control and a more generous seam allowance (Fig. 5.28).

Using the Shirring Attachment on Your Serger

Shirring attachments are available for most sergers with a differential feed (d.f.) because d.f. is needed to facilitate the shirring. For brand specific information ask your local dealer and refer to your Operating Manual. See the Sew-How tip in "Using the Gathering Foot on Your Sewing Machine" to determine how much your ruffle will gather.

1. Set your serger for a balanced three-thread overlock. Place the longer ruffle fabric under the foot right side up, and serge a couple of stitches, stopping with the needle in the fabric.

2. Raise the foot and place the shorter, flat fabric right side down, above the separator in the attachment and against the needle.

3. Lower the presser foot and serge so the lower layer feeds and gathers freely (Fig. 5.29).

Easiest Gathering Using Machine Adjustments
Needle-Tension Gathering Using Your Serger

For the quickest, easiest gathers using your serger, tighten your needle tensions. Use a long 3/4-thread stitch. On a test swatch, tighten needle tensions while serging until you achieve the desired effect.

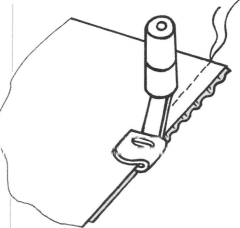

Fig. 5.28: *Place fabric to be gathered under the foot, right side up; then lower the foot. Slip the flat piece into the slot, right side down and sew.*

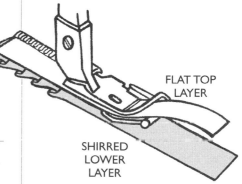

Fig. 5.29: *Place fabric to be gathered under the foot right side up and serge a couple of stitches. Raise the foot and place the flat fabric right side down above the separator and against the needle; serge.*

FLAT TOP LAYER

SHIRRED LOWER LAYER

"Ease-Plusing" Using Your Sewing Machine

Ease-plusing can be done on your sewing machine. First, overcast the raw edge, then set your machine for a straight stitch and a stitch length appropriate for the fabric. Then place your finger behind the foot and hold the fabric firmly while sewing ¼" (6mm) away from the edge. Continue in this way until you can't hold the fabric any longer; release, then continue as before. This is called "ease-plusing."

Differential-Feed "Ease-Plusing" Using Your Serger

For sergers that have the differential feed (d.f.) feature, dial it to the plus setting and follow the instructions above for ease-plusing with your sewing machine. The d.f. can also be used in combination with tightening the needle tension.

EASY EMBELLISHMENTS FOR STUNNING SURFACES

Fabric color and surface design give pillows personality. The designs in our book are as simple as fashioning a pillow out of antique linens — where the time-consuming embroidery was done by someone else's hand — and as complicated as making interchangeable eyes, noses, and mouths, thereby turning a plain pillow into the ultimate in pillow personality (Fig. 5.30). This last section explains the easiest and most professional ways to create the surface designs we've used, while playing with a variety of today's sewing tools and the sewing machine and serger accessories you've always wanted to try. Remember that, in most cases, the pillow front and back should be decorated *before* they are sewn together.

Creative Couching

Add texture and personality by laying down thread, cord, lace, ribbon, sequins, soutache, serged braid, etc., and attaching (or couching) it to a foundation fabric.

1. Thread your sewing machine with an all-purpose thread that matches whatever you are couching to the foundation. If you're using several colors for the couched cord, use monofilament thread top and bobbin. If someone's face will end up on this couched pillow, use thread matching the foundation fabric through the needle, and monofilament on the bobbin, so the monofilament won't scratch.

2. Using your piping or embroidery foot, set your zigzag stitch just wide enough to clear whatever you are couching to the foundation, and a two-stitch length (13 stitches per inch) (Fig. 5.31). Couch down wider ribbons and braids using a decorative stitch.

Make Your Own Serger Braid

When you can't find the braid you want, raid your ribbon and thread collection and make serger braid. Use a balanced three-thread or flatlock stitch with decorative thread in the upper looper, or stitch a rolled edge over a filler cord.

First decide on the desired braid width, choose the appropriate filler cord, and stitch.

- For **narrow braid filler,** use one or more strands of pearl or crochet cotton and the rolled hem.
- For **wider braid filler,** use Seams Great (nylon tricot cut in 1/2" [1.3cm] widths), or nylon tricot cut 1/2" (1.3cm) with the stretch (being sure to stretch it while serging). Also try ribbon floss or 1/4" (6mm) ribbon as filler cord.

1. Thread your upper looper with a decorative thread (e.g., Woolly Nylon, Candlelight, #8 pearl cotton, or Decor 6); thread needle and lower looper with all-purpose serger thread. Set your serger for a three-thread flatlock or balanced overlock stitch and a short stitch length (Fig. 5.32).

   SERGING SAVVY: *To make fusible braid, use a fusible thread such as ThreadFuse in the lower looper.*

2. Thread filler cord over the toe and under the back of the foot.

   SERGING SAVVY: *Some sergers have helpful cord guides built into the standard foot. The pearl/beading or sequin foot will keep extra-fat filler cord straight.*

3. Serge over the filler cord for the desired stitch density and texture. If you have used fusible thread in the lower looper, arrange the serger braid in a pleasing design and fuse it onto the foundation fabric following the manufacturer's instructions and using a press cloth. Then couch over it with your sewing machine (see Fig. 5.31), so it can withstand the ordinary wear and tear of a pillow fight. If you have not used fusible thread on your lower looper, couch down serger braid (see Fig. 5.32) as described in "Creative Couching" earlier in this chapter.

Fig. 5.32: *Serger braid made by serging over ribbon floss, narrow-cut tricot, or elastic cord. Use decorative thread in the upper looper and multi-purpose threads in the lower looper and needle.*

Fabric Tubes Made Fast and Fun

Have you avoided making spaghetti straps or fabric button loops because you didn't like to turn them? Then you need to know about the Fasturn system or how to turn a tube using your serger thread chain to pull it through.

Fasturn Sewing Machine Method

Designer Sandra Benfield strip-pieced tubes by butting them together and joining them with decorative machine stitches (see the Designer Showcase Key and the color pages). To use the Fasturn:

1. Cut fabric strips twice the width needed, plus 1/2" (1.3cm) for seam allowances (e.g., for a 1" (2.5cm) flat finished tube, cut your fabric strip the desired length and 2 1/2" (6.5cm) wide).

   SEW-HOW: *For tubes that can be shaped into curves, cut the fabric on the bias and sew a seam using a one-width, one-length (24 stitches per inch) zigzag. Then stitches won't pop.*

2. Fold the fabric strip in half the long way, right sides together, and stitch a 1/8" (3mm) seam the length of the tube and across one

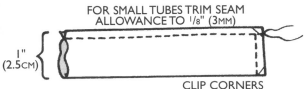

1"
(2.5CM)

CLIP CORNERS

Fig. 5.33: *Fold the fabric strip in half the long way and seam the length and across the end of the tube.*

FOLD FABRIC END
OVER TUBE OPENING

Fig. 5.34: *Slip the fabric tube over the long brass tube until the closed end is tight against the brass tube opening.*

Fig. 5.35: *Insert the hook. Holding the tube in one hand, ease the fabric toward the end. Begin pulling the hook handle and pull wire straight out of the brass tube.*

end (Fig. 5.33). Ends may be left open if a finished end isn't needed.

3. Slip the fabric tube over the long brass tube until the closed end of the fabric tube is tight against the brass tube. If the end of the tube is open, fold the end of the fabric tube over the end of the brass tube just enough to cover the opening; then hold it tight (Fig. 5.34).

4. Insert the hook into the brass tube from the open handle-end. Holding the fabric taut over the end of the tube, push the hook point through the fabric while twisting the hook to the right until the entire hook is through.

5. Holding the tube with one hand, ease the fabric toward the turning end. As you begin pulling the hook handle with the other hand, pull the wire straight out of the tube (Fig. 5.35). Remove the hook by untwisting the end. When you buy a Fasturn, you will receive a detailed instruction manual with several fool-proof tips and suggestions for use. Remember to register your Fasturn set and receive periodic newsletters and product updates.

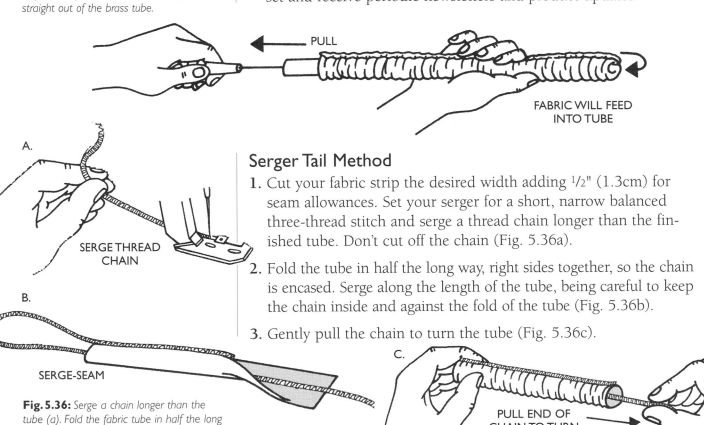

PULL

FABRIC WILL FEED
INTO TUBE

A.

SERGE THREAD
CHAIN

B.

SERGE-SEAM

Fig. 5.36: *Serge a chain longer than the tube (a). Fold the fabric tube in half the long way, so that the chain is encased (b). Pull chain to turn the tube (c).*

Serger Tail Method

1. Cut your fabric strip the desired width adding ½" (1.3cm) for seam allowances. Set your serger for a short, narrow balanced three-thread stitch and serge a thread chain longer than the finished tube. Don't cut off the chain (Fig. 5.36a).

2. Fold the tube in half the long way, right sides together, so the chain is encased. Serge along the length of the tube, being careful to keep the chain inside and against the fold of the tube (Fig. 5.36b).

3. Gently pull the chain to turn the tube (Fig. 5.36c).

C.

PULL END OF
CHAIN TO TURN

Flatlocking Most Fabulous

For a decorative topstitch, flatlock the edge of a free-flowing appliqué (see Linda Wisner's appliquéd Ultrasuede Patchwork Pillow in the color pages and in the Designer Showcase Key).

Two-Thread Flatlock

Some sergers can use two threads to stitch a flatlock (check your Operating Manual). To do this, thread one needle and one looper for a two-thread overedge. Set for a balanced stitch and serge along the cut or folded edge. Because the two-thread overedge doesn't lock at the seamline, the flatlock automatically opens when you pull it flat. In Tammy Young and Lori Bottom's *ABCs of Serging*, they explain that "the looper thread lies on top of the fabric while the needle thread is pulled to the edge on the underside. Because the two threads don't form a locking stitch at the needleline, it is called an 'overedge' rather than an 'overlock.'"

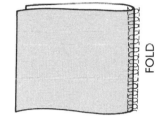

Three-Thread Flatlock

For the widest flatlock, thread the left needle and the upper and lower loopers; set stitch length for a short- to medium-width stitch. Loosen the needle tension almost to zero, and tighten the lower looper until the thread forms a straight line on the right side of the stitch. Guide the fabric fold or cut edges so the fabric fills half the width of the stitch (Fig. 5.37).

Fig. 5.37: *To flatlock, guide the fabric halfway under the foot so that the fabric fills half of the stitch. Serge, then pull stitches flat.*

Free-Machine Embroidery Made Easy

Using your darning foot and monofilament thread top and bobbin, lower the feed dogs, and set your machine for a straight stitch. Lower the presser foot and take one stitch, pulling the bobbin thread to the surface of the fabric. Take several stitches in one place, then cut thread tails off at the fabric and continue. Free-machine embroidery not only holds little scraps of fabrics, ribbons, and laces in place, but it takes the place of heavy stitches around appliqués.

Perfect Pleats

Designer Annie Tuley used the Perfect Pleater to make her Twisted Ribbon Pillow (see the Designer Showcase Key and the color pages). Look for The Perfect Pleater through your local fabric retailer or mail-order source.

1. Place the pleater on a table or counter top at least as long and somewhat wider than the pleater and with the louver openings pointing away from you. Your fabric should be in front of you on the surface of the table so that the weight of the unpleated fabric will not pull out tucks already in the pleater.

2. With the fabric *right side down,* use your fingers to tuck the fabric into the louvers. Using a credit card, push the fabric into each louver, sliding the edge of the card along the length of the louver. Repeat this until you have the desired number of pleats (Fig. 5.38).

Fig. 5.38: *With the fabric right side down, use your fingers to tuck the fabric into the louvers until you have the desired number of pleats.*

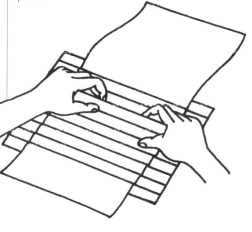

SEW-HOW: *For wider pleats, skip every other louver.*

3. Fuse a light-weight interfacing, such as fusible tricot, to the pleats following the interfacing manufacturer's instructions (Fig. 5.39). Let the fabric cool; then remove tucked fabric from the pleater by gently rolling the pleater to open the louvers.

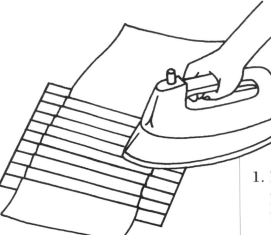

Fig. 5.39: *Press, then fuse, interfacing to the back of the pleats. Remove tucked fabric from pleater by gently rolling the pleater to open the louvers.*

Quilting Quips

Designer Donna Babylon machine quilted the center section of her pillow (see the Designer Showcase Key and on the color pages).

1. Make a quilt sandwich by layering a top fabric and batting and pin the sandwich together. (We like to work out the design and technique on a test swatch first.)

SEW-HOW: *To make two Double Diagonal pillows, cut top fabric and batting twice as large as needed or 9" (23cm) by twice the diagonal measurement of the pillow, then cut it apart.*

2. Using all-purpose thread top and bobbin, set your machine for a straight or decorative stitch, and use your embroidery or appliqué foot. (If your machine stitches the extra-wide embroidery designs, use the wide foot it requires because it displaces more pressure over a larger area for better results.) Most machines have a quilting bar that comes as a standard accessory. Place this on your machine as described in your Operating Manual and move it out the distance desired. This guide will help keep your quilting rows straight and an even distance from each other. Cut your quilting piece and use it as a decorative pillow inset.

SEW-HOW: *If you have a walking foot with a quilting bar attached, use the walking foot to prevent fabric distortion and to keep the underlayer from coming up short.*

Ultimate Ultrasuede

Pillows don't require a lot of this luxurious and easy-to-care-for fabric, but there are some tricks. For creative pillow ideas, see Nancy Zieman's and Linda Wisner's pillows in the Designer Showcase Key and on the color pages. Here are some tips:

- Use a size 75/11 stretch needle to prevent skipped stitches.
- Use a Teflon presser foot. The underside is smooth, so it offers the most support around the needle, which prevents puckering and skipped stitches. It also helps both fabric layers feed evenly, so one seam doesn't come up short.
- If you still have skipped stitches, use far left or far right needle position to correct it.
- Use fine silk pins or a glue stick to hold seams and prevent perforating the fabric.
- For fine, drapeable faux suedes and leathers, use a conventional method of seaming with right sides together.
- For heavier Ultrasuede, overlap the seam. First cut out the project with 5/8" (1.5cm) seam allowances. Then dot the glue stick along the back side of the seam. Lay glue stick side over the other edge, overlapping the seam allowance. Topstitch a presser foot width or less from the cut edge. Stitch a second topstitch a presser foot width or less away from the first. Trim excess seam allowance to the stitching.
- To press, use a chamois press cloth (available through mail-order sources). Wet the press cloth, then ring out as much water as possible. The chamois cloth holds in the moisture for a good press while protecting the surface of the fabric.

We hope you've been inspired enough by these "pillow personality" treatments, techniques, and embellishments to use them in your upcoming pillow projects. They'll also work well in your other sewing and embellishing endeavors. In Chapter Five look for pillow construction basics, from the "Fabric Fundamentals" to making "Perfect Pillow Corners."

Chapter 6

THE PILLOW PRIMER

Provisions and Procedures for Praiseworthy Pillows

While Chapter Five showed you many ways to add pizzazz to your pillows, this chapter gets down to basics. First we'll cover the materials used to create a pillow — both the essentials and the many optional tools that will make construction a breeze. Then we'll describe some innovative techniques for putting together the basic pillow components. If you gather the proper provisions and learn these easy-as-pie procedures, your pillows are guaranteed to be beyond par.

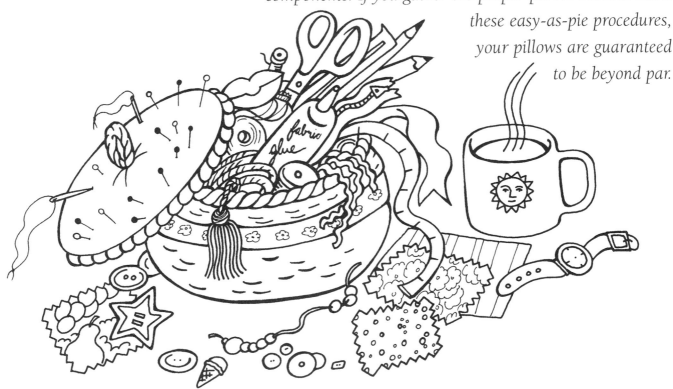

PILLOW PROVISIONS: EVERY GOOD PILLOW IS THE SUM OF ITS PARTS

To create a pleasing pillow, you need the right materials and the right tools to manipulate them. Whether it's thread, stuffing, or the machines that stitch them together, choosing your provisions carefully helps ensure pillow perfection.

Machine Mastery

Several techniques used in pillow making can be done without a machine. Good examples are no-sew fusing and tying, as well as hand-sewing for sewing on buttons, attaching heirloom trims, closing an opening after a pillow has been stuffed, and restitching a small split. For other projects you'll need a sewing machine. If you don't have one, there are always used machines available to rent or borrow through your local sewing machine dealers. New, quality low- to mid-priced machines are available, too. Although you can find used machines to buy through the newspaper or flea market, you won't get the service or instruction you would by buying it from a reputable sewing machine dealer, so check there first.

Throughout this book you will also see instructions for a serger. If this is a new term to you, a serger is a machine for home use that simultaneously sews the seam, overcasts the raw edges together, then cuts off the excess seam allowance. It can also be used for speedy edge finishing and decorative techniques. While the serger isn't necessary for the pillows in this book, we give you serging options, which are often faster and more professional looking than the techniques done with the sewing machine. Sergers also have a variety of accessory feet available to help you insert piping, zippers, and to shirr and gather ruffles.

Fabric Fundamentals

Find the fiber content, fabric width, pattern repeat, and recommended cleaning method on the bolt-end. Although many home decorator fabrics are 100% cotton and can be washed, washing often ruins the fabric finish. You'll also find that decorator trims may also be constructed of washable fibers but the recommended care instructions are "Dry Clean Only." Therefore, make your pillow covers removable where decorator fabrics and trims are used, and dry-clean to preserve the fabric finish and prevent uneven shrinking. If you are using fashion fabric and trims, pre-shrink them as you would for garment sewing so that the pillow or pillow cover is washable.

Thoughts on Thread

Whether selecting thread for your sewing machine or serger, read the label, unwrap a little, then take a close look at it. With the exception of Woolly Nylon, which has a crimped texture, it should have a smooth, even appearance. For your sewing machine, *all-purpose sewing thread* is generally three-ply and heavier than all-purpose serger thread. Serger thread is available on cones or tubes of 1,000 to 6,000 yards and is generally a two-ply and lighter weight than conventional all-purpose sewing thread. This way the several strands of lightweight thread used in a serged seam keep the fabric and seam supple.

Monofilament thread is like very fine fishline and blends with other thread or fiber colors, which means that you don't have to rethread your machine or serger when using different color fabrics on the same project. The best monofilament thread we've found is 100% polyester and is .004mm in diameter — very fine for soft pliable results. Use monofilament on your sewing machine for couching; use it in your serger for invisible hemming, or for flatlocking to couch over ribbon, sequins, and pearls.

Presser Feet Pointers

Because pillow-making lends itself to the practical and creative uses of both sewing machine and serger presser feet, we find the following are as helpful as they are fun to use.

Sewing Machine Presser Feet

- appliqué/embroidery
- pearls and piping*
- zipper foot
- blindhem/edgestitch
- standard zigzag
- buttonhole (sliding or standard)

Serger (2/3- or 3/4-thread) Presser Feet

- standard
- blindhem*
- piping foot*
- rolled-hem foot (sometimes you need a rolled-hem plate, too)

not usually a standard accessory foot; check with your local dealer for availability for your make and model

Other Pillow Prerequisites

Here are some basic tools that will help ensure your pillow making success.

Sewing and Serging Tools

- good quality pins (we like fine glass-head quilting pins; they are sharp, longer, and stronger than regular pins); use fine silk pins for silks and heirloom fabrics such as organdy and batiste
- bodkin or ribbon threader to pull elastic through a casing
- pin cushion, pin box, or magnetic pin cushion
- hand needle (for hand basting and tacking down trims) and a thimble
- new sewing machine needles from sizes 70/10 - 100/16 for most jobs (see Tables at back of book)
- cutting and clipping scissors
- rotary cutter and board (optional, but nice to have)

Measuring Tools

- measuring tape
- seam gauge
- yardstick or transparent 6" × 24" (15cm × 61cm) ruler

Marking Tools

- water-erasable or disappearing (air-soluble) marking pens (to mark light-colored fabrics)
- erasable quilting pencil (Jackie's favorite is silver in color because it marks well on both light and dark fabrics)
- pocket-former to use as a template for marking pillow corners and curves

Tools for Stuffing Loose Fiberfill

- hemostats (available in drug or medical supply stores) — for grabbing and pushing loose fiberfill exactly where you need it
- Stuff-It tool — to push fiberfill into corners
- wooden spoon — to scoop and load loose fiberfill or styrofoam pellets into a stitched pillow shape

Pressing and Ironing Tools

- steam iron
- press cloth (for placing on the right side of the fabric to prevent the iron from creating shine)
- paper removed from large pieces of paper-backed fusible web to use as a non-stick press cloth for fusible webs and iron-on flexible vinyl (see description for Teflon Pressing Sheet).
- Teflon Pressing Sheet — a small, translucent, non-stick pressing sheet used to prevent fusible adhesive from sticking to the iron and/or the ironing surface. Use it with fusible web, paper-backed fusible web, liquid fusible web, or as a press cloth on fabrics that need lower iron temperatures such as rayon braid.

Pillow Forms and Other "Stuff"

Pillow forms are time-saving fabric-covered pillows that are a given size and shape — ready to pop into a decorative pillow cover. Pillow forms come in a variety of sizes and shapes, with new ones being introduced all the time. Choose forms that suit your style. Stuffing can be made of different fiber contents, the most common being 100% polyester or a cotton/poly blend. What determines the weight of the pillow and "squeezability" is how the fiber is made.

Hollow-core polyester fibers hold air inside, providing loft and recovery without the weight or bulk of solid-core fiberfill — so it's the air in the fiber that keeps the pillow fluffy. Solid polyester fibers are more rigid, and heavier than hollow-core fibers, giving you a more tailored look. Budget polyester fiberfill can be lumpy. Personal preference will lead you to the best decision. Read the pillow form packaging, compare brands for squeezability, and decide how you want to care for your pillow. Look for pillow forms by Air-Lite Synthetics, Fairfield Processing, Morning Glory, and Sterns Manufacturing (Mountain Mist).

Loose fiberfill is used to stuff odd-shaped pillows, three-dimensional shapes, toys, and dolls.

Styrofoam pellets work well for large floor pillows because they are light enough to lift and move around and conform to the body laying on it. Find pellets or styrofoam "popcorn" through your local mail-service store.

Time-Saving Tricks of the Trade

Although the items described in this section are not essential, they provide you with many ways to amplify your pillow making skills. Some of these items are considered "notions" and are found grouped together on the wall around the perimeter of a fabric store. The fusible interfacings and stabilizers are often found in the craft or home decorating departments within a fabric store.

Fusible fleece adds strength, durability, and dimension to a pillow top.

Fusible knit interfacing stabilizes or reinforces fabrics to withstand the wear and tear of family living. We like fusible knit interfacing because it is lightweight yet strong. Look for Pellon's Easy-Knit, HTC's Fusi-Knit, and Knit Fuse by Dritz.

Iron-on flexible vinyl makes fabric waterproof — it's great for patio furniture, tote bags, place mats, tablecloths, shower curtains, children's gift items, slipcovers, and pillows. Fuse this product to a piece of fabric following the manufacturer's instructions. Some brands can be fused to each other and can be written on or painted on as well. Look for Heat'nBond Iron-on Flexible Vinyl, and Kittrich Iron-on Clear Cover.

Paper-backed fusible web is available by the yard or cut into 1/4" (6mm) - 3/4" (2cm) widths. Just iron it on paper side up (following the manufacturer's instructions), peel off the paper, then fuse up a hem or attach trim or ribbons. Fusible web makes any fabric fusible, so it's great for patching and appliqué; look for Aleene's Hot Stitch, Heat'nBond Lite, Magic Fuse, HTC's TransWeb, and Pellon's Wonder-Under.

Glue sticks are used to temporarily glue-baste an appliqué, zipper, or button in place.

Permanent washable glue is used to hold knotted ends, and other bits and pieces in pillows. Look for washable (but not always dry-cleanable) clear solvent-based glues called EZ's Fabric Glue, Beacon's Fabri Tak, Fabric Mender by Magic, Liquid Stitch by Dritz, and Plexi 400 Stretch Adhesive. White, waterproof glues to look for are Aleene's OK-to-Wash-It, Glu-N-Wash, or Unique Stitch.

Res-Q Tape is a paper-backed double-faced tape that holds fabric to fabric. Use it to eliminate "gaposis" at an envelope closure on a pillow back, between blouse buttons, and to temporarily hold hems that have ripped out (it's a must for any desk drawer at work).

Seam sealant is a clear or white liquid that is dotted on the end of threads to prevent them from raveling. Also use seam sealant on the cut edge of ribbon or trim or in the cutting space between the rows of stitches in a buttonhole, letting it dry before cutting the buttonhole open. Look for Fray Check, Stop Fraying, and Fray Stoppa in your local fabric or sewing machine store.

Tear-away stabilizer is paper-like yardage to use under fabric that will be embroidered. It prevents the stitches from puckering and creating a tunnel under the stitching. Look for Clotilde's No Whiskers, HTC's perforated Easy-Stitch, Pellon's Stitch 'N Tear or Tear-Away brands, and Sulky's iron-on tear-away stabilizer called Totally Stable.

Wash-away stabilizer is made of either a semi-transparent film or a strong lightweight fabric that dissolves in water. Sulky's Solvy, Speed Stitch's Wash-Away and Clotilde's Solv-it are transparent enough to trace over a design and onto the film. Then, once placed onto the right side of the fabric, it will wash or spritz away after stitching. Madeira's Melt-A-Way and HTC's Rinsaway are strong lightweight fabrics that dissolve in water.

PILLOW PROCEDURES: PUTTING YOU THROUGH YOUR PILLOW PACES

Even if you've only browsed through this book, you already know that pillows have come a long way from two squares of fabric sewn together. Yet, almost every pillow — regardless of its shape, size, or function — still relies on a fabric shell that needs to be measured, sewn (or fused or serged) together, stuffed, and closed up. In this part of the primer, we offer innovative techniques for pillow making, showing you the best ways to: measure fabric to fit the pillow form; create smooth and even corners when sewing the fabric shell; construct durable (but easy-to-sew) closures for pillow covers, and add hems and edges to pillow components. All of the techniques described are fast, fun, and provide the perfect finishing touches to your pillow projects.

Measure It: Pillow Dimension Guidelines

If you plan to use a pre-made pillow form, measure it first from seam to seam across the middle. Even though the package may say 16" (40.5cm) square or round, dimensions do vary slightly, even within the same manufacturer. If the pillow form is too large for your pillow cover, the fabric will stretch, causing lines across the pillow similar to too-tight clothing — not very attractive.

When using soft, "squeezable" pillow forms, cut your pillow cover fabric the exact size of the pillow, then use 1/2" (6mm) seam allowances all the way around. For example, cut your pillow cover fabric 16" (40.5cm) in diameter to comfortably cover a 16" (40.5cm) round pillow form.

For firmer, more tailored pillow forms, cut the pillow cover the pillow dimensions plus 1" (2.5cm) for seam allowances. For example,

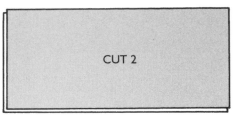

CUT 2

TWICE PILLOW LENGTH PLUS
4" (10CM)

Fig. 6.1: *Cut two back envelope pieces the width of and double the length of the pillow plus 4" (10cm).*

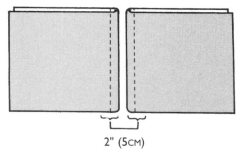

2" (5CM)

Fig. 6.2: *Fold each fabric strip in half the short way, then topstitch a presser-foot width from the fold on each envelope piece.*

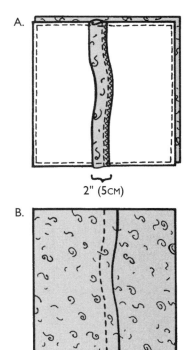

A.

2" (5CM)

B.

2" (5CM)

Fig. 6.3: *Place pillow top and envelope pieces right sides together and overlapping envelope hems.*

to cover a 16" (40.5cm) square pillow form, cut your fabric 17" (43cm) square, and use 1/4" (6mm) seam allowances all the way around. The narrower seam allowances reduce bulk in the seams for a smooth finish.

Envelop It: Making the Basic Envelope

Save time and materials by decorating only one side of your pillow cover; then make it easy-care with an envelope closure. First, cut your top pillow piece as described in "Measure It: Pillow Dimension Guidelines" earlier in this chapter. Decorate or embellish your pillow top. (Find inspiration and general instructions in Chapters One through Four and the Designer Showcase color pages). Then follow the instructions that apply to the weight of fabric you're using.

Envelope Closures Using Lightweight Fabric

A doubled back envelope has more body and will wear better when using lightweight fabrics.

1. Cut two back envelope pieces the width of and double the length of the pillow, plus 4" (10cm), as shown in Fig. 6.1. For a 16" (40.5cm) square pillow, cut each pillow back 16" × 36" (40.5cm × 91.5cm).

2. Fold each fabric strip in half the short way; then topstitch a presser-foot width from the fold on each envelope piece (Fig. 6.2).

3. Place pillow top and envelope pieces, right sides together so envelope hems overlap each other approximately 2" (5cm). Raw edges of pillow top and envelope are even around the perimeter of the pillow cover (Fig. 6.3).

4. Stitch pillow top to envelope back. Open, turn cover right side out, and pop in your pillow form.

Envelope Closures for Heavier Fabrics (or When You Don't Have Enough Fabric to Make a Double Envelope Back)

1. Cut two back envelope pieces the width of and half the length of the pillow plus 4" (10cm), as shown in Fig. 6.4. For a 16" (40.5cm) pillow cut each envelope piece 16" × 12" (40.5 × 30.5cm).

2. Finish and hem one narrow end of each envelope piece by either fusing, overcasting, or serge-finishing and then topstitching or by serging a rolled edge (see "Give it an Edge: Hems and Edges How-To's" later in this chapter).

3. If you don't want the opening to gap after the pillow form is in, close by hand stitching or:
   - use a not-too-big pillow form
   - stick a strip of Res-Q-Tape between the hemmed edges (Fig. 6.5a)
   - attach snap tape, or hook-and-loop tape fastener to envelope opening (Figs. 6.5b and 6.5c)

- make a buttonhole closure (Fig. 6.5d)
- close with a zipper (see Figs. 6.21 and 6.22)

4. Place pillow top and envelope pieces, right sides together so envelope hems overlap each other approximately 2" (5cm). Raw edges of pillow top and envelope are even around the perimeter of the pillow cover (see Fig. 6.3).

5. Stitch pillow top to envelope back. Open, turn cover right side out, and pop in your pillow form.

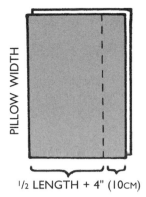

Fig. 6.4: *Cut two back envelope pieces the width of and half the length of the pillow plus 4" (10cm).*

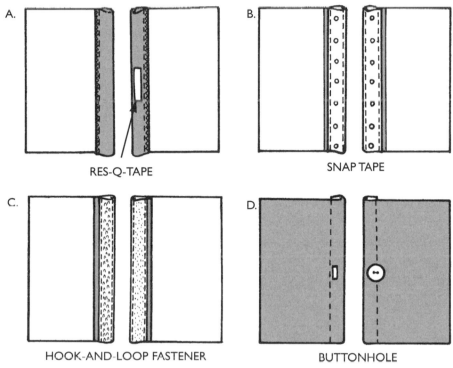

A. RES-Q-TAPE

B. SNAP TAPE

C. HOOK-AND-LOOP FASTENER

D. BUTTONHOLE

Fig. 6.5: *Prevent envelope closure from pulling open — attach snap tape, hook and loop fastener, or close with a button and a buttonhole. For a no-sew option, close using double-faced Res-Q-Tape.*

Corner It: Perfect Pillow Corners

Square pillows often end up with "funny ears" or unintentionally exaggerated corners. Use our Corner Tapering Trick to create smooth, even corners.

Corner Tapering Trick

1. Place pillow back and front pieces right sides together.

2. Using a fabric marker and ruler, measure in 1/2" (1.3cm) from the seam allowance intersection at each corner, tapering lines out to the edge one-fourth the side length of the pillow.

3. When you are ready, sew or serge the back and front pieces together, using a 1/2" (1.3cm) seam allowance and stitching along the tapering lines at the corners.

SEW-HOW: *For a curved square corner, trace around a pocket former curve so all eight (pillow fronts and backs) corners are uniform (Fig. 6.6). Also refer to Fig. 5.6 in Chapter Five when attaching cord or piping at a corner.*

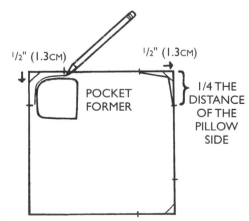

Fig. 6.6: *Trace around a pocket-former curve so that all corners are uniform.*

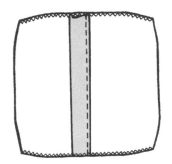

Fig. 6.7: *With right sides together, serge-seam opposite sides of the pillow cover.*

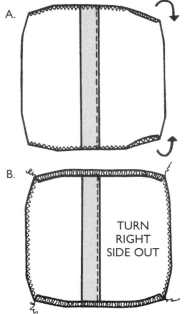

Fig. 6.8: *Wrap and press the finished seams in toward the pillow top and serge-seam the other two sides.*

Fig. 6.9: *Comfortably stuff small center square with loose fiberfill. Machine-stitch the opening closed.*

Serged and Wrapped Corners

Serge a square pillow without piping using a wide balanced three-thread or 3/4-thread overlock stitch and wrapping the corners:

1. Mark and taper corners, following steps 1 and 2 on page 71.

2. Place front and back envelope pillow pieces right sides together and serge-seam opposite sides of the pillow cover (Fig. 6.7).

3. Press both seams flat; then fold or wrap and press the seam allowances in toward the pillow top and serge-seam the other two sides (Fig. 6.8). Turn pillow cover right side out through the envelope opening.

Jan's Easy Mitered Corners

To make a mitered flange pillow, do this:

1. Cut pillow back three times larger than the pillow front plus 1" (2.5cm) for hem allowances (e.g., for a 7" [18cm] square center medallion pillow front, cut the pillow back 22" [53.5cm] square).

2. Press a 1/4" (6mm) hem allowance around the perimeter of the back square. Press to wrong side.

   SERGING SAVVY: *Eliminate seam allowances on pillow flange and either use a wide, balanced three-thread overlock with decorative threads in the upper and lower loopers or serge a narrow rolled edge around the square.*

3. Center smaller front square on the larger pillow back, wrong sides together and sew around three-and-a-half sides. Stuff small center square with loose fiberfill using hemostats or a wooden spoon and Stuff-It tool to push fiberfill where needed. Don't overstuff. Machine-stitch to close the opening (Fig. 6.9).

4. Fold one side of the backing toward the front, so the hem or finished edge of the flange covers the stitching from step three. Repeat for the other three sides. Press and crease the flange fold all the way around (Fig. 6.10).

5. Open flange; in each corner, fold a right-angle triangle with the long edge crossing the intersection of the folds. Tuck the triangle into the flange (Fig. 6.11). Press and topstitch around the flange. *Note:* We don't usually tack down the corners unless the pillow will have a lot of rough use, but if you want to, machine stitch, following the angle of the fold. (See Victoria Waller's pillow in the Designer Showcase Key and in the color pages).

FOLD AND CREASE

Fig. 6.10: *Fold backing toward the front so the finished edge covers the stitching.*

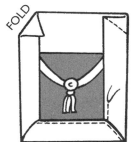

Fig. 6.11: *Open the fold. In each corner, fold a right-angle triangle and tuck it in the flange. Press and topstitch around the center medallion.*

Jackie's Pillowcase Flange

To make the easiest flange pillow cover:

1. Cut two squares 5" (12.5cm) longer and 5" (12.5cm) wider than your square pillow form. For example, for a 16" (40cm) pillow form, cut two 21" (52cm) squares.

2. Place right sides together and sew or serge around three-fourths of the pillow, using ¼" (6mm) seam allowances. Press a ¼" (6mm) hem all the way around the opening (Fig. 6.12). Turn pillow case right side out, and press again.

    SERGING SAVVY: *For a decorative flange, machine-baste wrong sides together ¹/4" (6mm) from the raw edge. Thread upper and lower loopers with decorative thread and serge-finish around three edges with a wide balanced three-thread overlock.*

3. Center the pillow form in the pillow case, pinning next to the pillow's edge. Machine stitch around the perimeter of the pillow form using your zipper foot (Fig. 6.13). For more pizzazz zigzag over decorator cord.

4. Pin opening closed, edgestitch or decoratively serge-finish across the opening. If you are edgestitching, continue around the perimeter of the flange. Decorate the pillow with tassels or ribbon bows (Fig. 6.14).

Give It an Edge: Hems and Edges How-To's

We use three types of pillow hems and one quick edge finish for the pillows in this book:

- fused no-sew hems
- finished, turned, and topstitched hems
- ready-in-a-minute rolled hems
- straightest edgestitching

Fused No-Sew Hems

For a quick, permanent hem on a ruffle, or to finish the opening of an envelope pillow back, fuse it using a paper-backed fusible web.

1. Using the paper side up, lay ½"- (1.3cm) wide fusible web strip on the hem edge and fuse following the manufacturer's instructions. Let the paper cool; then use your scalloping or pinking shears and pink the hem edge. Remove the release paper.

2. Turn the hem up ¼" (6mm) and press, again following the manufacturer's instructions (Fig. 6.15). Fusing a hem to fusible web gives a strong, permanent fuse.

Fig. 6.12: *Press a ¹/4" (6mm) hem all the way around the open side.*

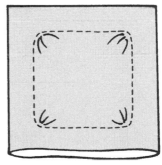

Fig. 6.13: *Center pillow and machine-stitch around the perimeter of the pillow form.*

DECORATE WITH RIBBON ROSES

EDGESTITCH AROUND AND CLOSE

Fig. 6.14: *Edgestitch across the opening and around the perimeter of the flange.*

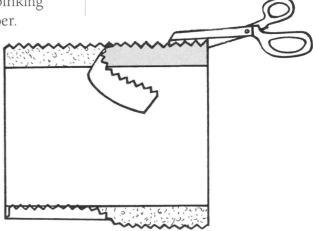

Fig. 6.15: *For a No-Sew Hem, fuse on narrow paper-backed fusible web following manufacturer's instructions. Let the fabric cool; pink the edge, peel off the paper, and press up a ¹/4"-³/8" (6mm - 1cm) hem.*

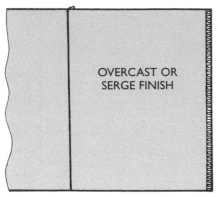

Fig. 6.16: *Overcast or serge-finish one of the wide ends of each envelope closure.*

1/4"–1/2" (6MM–13MM)

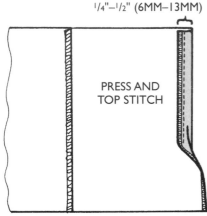

Fig. 6.17: *Turn back the finished edge the width of the stitch, then topstitch the hem a presser foot width from the fold with your sewing machine.*

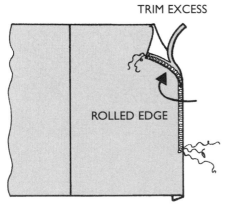

Fig.6.18: *If you don't have enough fabric for a generous hem, press a narrow 1/4"-1/2" (6mm - 1.3cm) hem, serge a rolled hem over the fold, and trim away the excess fabric.*

Finished, Turned, and Topstitched Hems

1. To *finish* a hem on an envelope closure, overcast the raw edge with one of the stitches on your sewing machine, or a balanced three-thread stitch on your serger (Fig. 6.16).

2. Turn back the finished edge the width of the stitch, then topstitch the hem a presser foot width from the fold with your sewing machine (Fig. 6.17).

Ready-In-A-Minute Rolled Hems

For the edge of a ruffle, pillow flange, or envelope closure, use the narrow rolled edge on your serger.

1. Set your serger for a rolled edge. Some sergers have a built-in rolled hem feature, which you adjust with a lever or dial. Others require changing the foot and/or needle plate. For information on stitching rolled hems with your serger, consult your Operating Manual.

2. Stitch a rolled edge on a single or double fabric layer using a matching thread color (Fig. 6.18). If necessary, trim the hem allowance away after serging.

Straightest Edgestitching

Edgestitching is a line of stitching 1/8" (3mm) or less from an edge and is generally stitched with thread matching the fabric. Edgestitch along strips and edges of fabrics you may have stitched on your pillow, using your blindhem or edgestitch foot.

1. Turn under and press the edge to be edgestitched. Place the edge of fold so it guides against the guide in the foot (Fig. 6.19).

2. Set your needle position so the needle is the desired distance from the edge and sew using a two- to three-length (9 - 13 stitches per inch) straight stitch.

Close It: No-Sew and Easy-Sew Closures
Knot, Tie, or Wrap-On Pillow Covers

The fastest, easiest way to change the look of a pillow is to pop a pillow form or an existing decorator pillow into two fabric squares such as napkins, hankies, or decorator fabric squares you have hemmed or serge-finished. Gail Brown, author of *Quick Napkin Creations* (Open Chain Publishing/Chilton, 1990) suggests knotting, tying, or wrapping napkin corners to cover a pillow (Fig. 6.20). In *Gail Brown's All-New Instant Interiors* (Open Chain Publishing/Chilton, 1992), she suggests wrapping a pillow with a 36" - 54" (91.5cm - 135cm) fabric square and securing the wrap with an Infinity Ring. Both of Gail's books are packed with great no-sew and easy-to-sew ideas for your home and fun gift ideas, too — a must for any sewing library.

Buttonhole Bytes

Although every sewing machine has its patented method of making buttonholes, these tips may give you a better-looking buttonhole.

- Make test buttonholes duplicating the fabric, interfacing, and fabric thicknesses of your project.

- Corded buttonholes look better and last longer. Many of today's buttonhole feet have a clip or clips to hold cording securely and so that you don't inadvertently sew through the cord. Cord buttonholes using multiple thread strands, pearl cotton, or embroidery floss. Jan needed white cord once and found that waxed dental floss worked great.

- When making buttonholes on soft fabric, narrow the width, lengthen the stitch, use a finer embroidery thread, and stabilize the wrong side of the fabric with either a tear-away or wash-away stabilizer.

- To prevent threads from unraveling, dribble a line of seam sealant between the cutting space; then let it dry before cutting the buttonhole open.

- For a prettier buttonhole, use 100% cotton mercerized thread top and bobbin, and slightly loosen the upper tension. The stitches lock on the underside of the fabric, causing the stitches on top to look smooth and rounded.

- Instead of buttonholes, use button loops, using the easy Fasturn method of making fabric tubes described in Chapter Five.

Goof-Proof Zippers

If you've avoided a project because it called for a zipper, you'll love our time-saving goof-proof zipper application. Some pillows simply need zipper closures because they get a lot of wear and tear, or need to look uniform both back and front. You can even make the zipper your focal point. *Remember to apply the zipper before attaching the pillow front to the back.* Once you've tried this application, you can successfully repeat it in about five minutes. . .no kidding!

1. Prepare pillow back as described in "Envelop It: Making the Basic Envelope" (see Figs. 6.1 - 6.5 and 6.15 - 6.19), so the overlap is approximately 2" (5cm).

2. Buy a zipper at least 2" (5cm) longer than width of the pillow back.

3. With the zipper closed and the pull out of the way, place the fold of the envelope underlap next to the zipper coil (Fig. 6.21) and stitch using your zipper foot.

4. Lightly spread fabric glue stick adhesive onto the other side of the zipper tape. Lay the envelope overlap over the zipper so the pillow edges are even. The glue stick adhesive temporarily holds the zipper in place.

5. With the right side of the envelope closure up, use your zipper or piping foot and decenter your needle (using the adjustable needle position function on your machine) so the stitches guide next to the zipper coil. The ridge under the piping foot or toe of the zipper foot will ride smoothly next to the coil, and because you have sewn the zipper in from the right side, your stitching is straight.

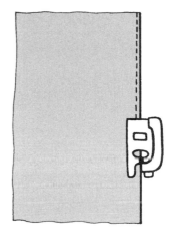

Fig. 6.19: *Place the edge of the fold so it guides against the guide in the foot. Set your needle position the desired distance from the edge and sew.*

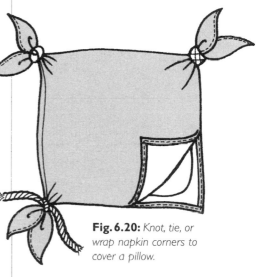

Fig. 6.20: *Knot, tie, or wrap napkin corners to cover a pillow.*

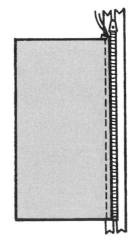

Fig. 6.21: *Place fold of the envelope underlap next to the zipper coil.*

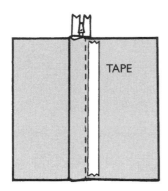

Fig. 6.22: *Use your zipper or piping foot and sew the second side of the zipper. To sew straight, place a strip of transparent tape next to the stitching line for easy guiding.*

SEW-HOW: *If you have trouble sewing straight, lay a strip of transparent tape next to the stitching line to use as a guide (Fig. 6.22).*

6. Move the zipper pull to the zipper's mid-point. Place front and back pillow pieces right sides together, and finish around the pillow as desired. Backstitch over the coil of the free ends of the zipper tape several times before cutting the excess zipper tape off and even with seam allowance.

Harmonious Hook-and-Loop Fasteners

Velcro is the most well-known brand of these handy closures. To attach them:

1. Cut the hook-and-loop tape the desired length.

2. Pin or glue-stick the loop side onto the fabric and sew around the perimeter with a 2.5 - 3 stitch length (9 stitches per inch), using a straight stitch.

3. Repeat step two for the hook side.

   SEW HOW: *Consider how your pillow will be used before you choose hook-and-loop fastener. You wouldn't want the hook side to snag or rub up against tender cheeks when it is not attached to the loop side.*

We hope you've enjoyed this handy sewing and serging guide, as well as the rest of the ideas in *Pillows! Pillows! Pillows!* We also hope our ideas will spark your imagination so that you become your own favorite designer. Thank you for reading our book. Look for more short subject topics in the *Sew & Serge* book series, available through your local sewing machine dealers, fabric stores, and your favorite mail-order catalogs. Until next time, happy creating.

J.D. and J. S

Doodle Page

POSSIBLE PILLOW PROJECTS

Pillow I'd Like to Make	For What Room or Special Purpose?	Page #	Sketch of Pillow
1.			
2.			
3.			
4.			
5.			

Table A–American and European Equivalent Needle Sizes

American	European	Suggested Fabrics
8	60	Silk chiffon, organza, sheers, fine cottons, and microfibers
9	65	Tissue faille, voile, georgette, blouse-weight silks, and microfibers
10	70	Blouse and lightweight dress fabric
11	75	Knit interlock, Lyrca activewear, knit sheers, Ultrasuede and other synthetic suedes and leathers, midweight microfibers
12	80	Suitweight silks, linens, and wools
14	90	Denim, topstitching with topstitching thread, heavy duck cloth, midweight real leather and suede
16	100	Very heavy duck cloth, some upholstery fabrics, upholstery vinyl
18	110	Some decorative hemstitching; use if the size 16/100 breaks
–	120	Decorative hemstitching; use if the size 18/110 breaks

Reprinted from *Jan Saunders' Wardrobe Quick-Fixes* (Radnor, PA: Chilton), 1995, p. 144.

Table B–Needle Point Types

Classification	Type
General Purpose Sewing Machine Needles	
15 × 1H 130/705H	**Universal:** Cross between a sharp point and a ballpoint tip used on most knits and wovens. This needle is most widely available and sews beautifully on the majority of fabrics. Twin-needle sizes available in 1.6 12/80, 2.0 12/80, 2.5 12/80, 3.0 12/80, 3.0 14/90, 4.0 12/80, 4.0 14/90, 6.0 16/100; triple needles available in 2.5 12/80 and 3.0 12/80.
15 × 1SP 130/705 SUK	**Ballpoint:** A round-tipped needle designed for use on heavy knits such as power net. The ball point slips easily between the loops in the knit fabric without skipping stitches or snagging. Not as widely available as the universal but available in sizes 10/70–16/100.
Blue Tip 130/705HS 130/705HPS (Pfaff) Sears "Q" Singer 2045	**Stretch:** Has a sharper point than a universal needle, with a deeper scarf; which aids in stitch formation to prevent skipped stitches. Recommended for swimwear knits, Lycra, synthetic suede, free-machine embroidery, and some microfibers. Often has a blue tip or shaft for easy identification. Twin-needle sizes available in 2.5 11/75 and 4.0 12/80.

Classification	Type

General Purpose Sewing Machine Needles (continued)

15 × 1DE
130/705HJ

Denim or Jeans: Sharp point to penetrate closely woven fabrics easily, without breaking. Recommended for denim, corduroy, and upholstery fabric. Single needles available in sizes 10/70-18/110. Twin needle sizes available in 4.0 16/100.

15 × 1 or 705B
(B for Bernina)
130/705 HM
Singer 2020
Microtex

Sharp or Pierce Point: A sharp needle used for sewing woven silks and microfibers. The small sizes (from 8/60-14/90) produce a very straight line of stitching. Also recommended for French hand sewing by machine on fine cottons and linen. Often has a violet shaft for easy identification. Bernina owners, read inside the hook cover to see if this needle is recommended for your machine.

Specialty Sewing Machine Needles

130/705 HM
Metafil

Embroidery: Designed for use with metallic, novelty, and machine embroidery threads; available in sizes 11/75 and 14/90. This needle has larger eye and groove dimensions to prevent threads from splitting and shredding. It also has a deeper scarf for better stitch formation and to prevent skipped stitches. The sharp point avoids damage to the fabric and other threads when embroidering. Often has a red shaft or band for easy identification. Twin-needle sizes available in 2.0 11/75 and 3.0 11/75.

705 Handicap

Handicap: *Sharp* point with a self-threading eye available in sizes 12/80 and 14/90.

130/705 HQ

Quilting: Durable tapered point for sewing the many seams required for piecing without damaging the fabric. Currently available in sizes 75 and 90. Often has a green shaft or band for easy identification.

130/705H
130/705HS
SPRING

Spring: Available in universal sizes 10/70-14/90, stretch 11/75 or 14/90, and denim 16/100, they have darning springs around them. Used for free-machine embroidery, darning, and quilting for better visibility. When using this needle, you don't need a darning foot.

15 × 1ST
130/705N

Topstitch: The eye and front groove of the needle are twice the size of a normal 11/75 or 14/90 needle to accommodate heavy topstitching thread. Some topstitching needles have sharp tips to produce the straightest topstitch.

15 × 1LL
130/705HLL
130/705NTW

Wedge Point or Leather: Available in sizes 10/70-18/110, this large-eye needle has a wedge point to penetrate leather. The point slices into the leather rather than perforating it.

130/705 H WING

Wing: The needle has wings running the length of the shaft to poke a large hole when hemstitching. The stitch goes in and out of the same hole, binding it open after stitching. Twin wing is available in size 16/100.

Reprinted from *Jan Saunders' Wardrobe Quick-Fixes* (Radnor, PA: Chilton), 1995, pp. 144-145.

Designer Showcase Key

If you agree, as we do, that two heads are better than one, then many heads are what we needed to bring you the latest and most innovative fabrics, threads, trims, and notions used in pillows today. So we asked fabric, trim, and pillow form companies as well as home decorating designers to add pillows to our Designer Showcase. Following is a description of each pillow in the designer's own words, with information about it, and the designer who contributed it.

Double Diagonal (upper left)

Machine quilting, piping, and shirred piping (ruching) is featured on the Double Diagonal pillow, which is geared to the intermediate sewer.

Product and fabric credits: *Hoffman Fabrics, Mountain Mist pillow form*

Skill level: *Intermediate*

Donna Babylon
Author of Pillow Pizzaz

Charted Needlework and Quilting (upper right)

This beginner/intermediate pillow includes charted needlework by machine, machine piecing, echo and twin needle quilting.

Product and fabric credits:
Sulky of America thread, Concord fabric

Skill level: *Beginner/intermediate*

Joyce Drexler
Promotion and Production Manager, Sulky of America

Ultra-Pillow (middle right and lower left)

This color-blocked pillow is a great first Ultrasuede project. You'll learn all the basics of working with synthetic suedes: marking, seaming, and topstitching.

Product and fabric credits: *Ultrasuede*

Skill level: *Beginner*

Nancy Zieman
President, Nancy's Notions, Ltd.

Ultrasuede Patchwork (lower right)

This pillow features a balanced three-thread stitch on edges of Ultrasuede pieces which are top stitched over home decorator fabric. It was featured in the book *Creative Serging for the Home and Other Quick Decorating Ideas* that Lynette Ranney Black and I wrote (Palmer/Pletsch Publishing).

Product and fabric credits: *Ultrasuede*

Skill level: *Intermediate*

Linda Wisner
*Author and designer,
Palmer/Pletsch
Publishing*

Easy And Elegant (middle left)

This is a variation of the "no-sew wrap-up" pillows shown in my book *Instant Interiors*. It is made from two 54" squares, right sides sewn together, then turned right-side out. Use either side out when it's tied over the pillow form.

Product and fabric credits: *Mill Creek and Rosebar fabric; Fairfield pop-in round pillow*

Skill level: *Beginner and above*

Gail Brown
Freelance author

Wavy Circle (upper left)

An intermediate level sew-er can machine quilt this on her machine. First draw the design on the pillow front. Add gathered cording and a scalloped ruffle.

Product and fabric credits: *Mountain Mist pillow form*

Skill level: *Intermediate*

Caryl Rae Hancock
Cutting Edge Designs (Art to Wear and Art Quilts; Classes on Machine Arts)

Medallion Pillow (middle)

This medallion pillow is stuffed with loose stuffing, decorated with ribbon, cording trim, a tassel, and a large brass-colored button.

Product and fabric credit:
Vickie Waller Designs, VIP Fabric (Christmas Orchard), Hollywood Trim tassel and cord, Streamline button, Offray ribbon

Skill level: *Beginner*

Victoria Waller
Home Decorating Product Manager, Prym-Dritz (Pillow submitted by Nancy Walsh)

Scrapbasket *(upper right)*

Beginners can make this pillow. Fabric on pillow front is top-stitched following the motifs. Although not shown, the fabric's border strip was put on the envelope back for an extra touch. Cording and a doubled ruffle line the pillow edges.

Product and fabric credits:
Quilts and Co. by Marti Mechell for Fabric Traditions
Skill level: *Beginner*

Ann Bulgrin
Merchandising coordinator, Fabric Traditions

Going Baroque *(lower right)*

There is no such thing as a right side to this fabric and both sides are used! Stitch the front panel to the pillow front and baste the bullion fringe to the back before construction of this intermediate level pillow.

Product and fabric credits:
Covington Fabrics Corp, Conso bullion fringe, Hollywood Trims, Fairfield pillow form
Skill level: *Intermediate*

Susan Voigt-Reising
Editor, Sewing Decor

Fringe Tapestry *(lower left)*

This pillow combines hand-stitching, machine sewing, and flatlocking on the serger. It is featured in *Creative Serging for the Home and Other Quick Decorating Ideas,* written by Linda Wisner and me (published by Palmer/Pletsch).

Product and fabric credits: *Hollywood Trim, Hobbs pillow form*
Skill level: *Intermediate*

Lynette Ranney Black
Author and teacher, Palmer/Pletsch Publishing

Quintessence *(upper left)*

A simple envelope with zipper and extended flap, this pillow can be made by an intermediate sewer. The shirring on the flap is made by zig-zagging over cord, the ribbon roses by wrapping and twisting while sewing by hand, then gluing them to the flap.

Product Credit: *Fairfield's Soft Touch pillow form, Aleene's Tacky Glue*
Skill level: *Intermediate*

Shirley J. Fomby
Regional Sales Manager, Fairfield Processing Corp.

PHOTO COURTESY OF RON FOMBY

Decorative Tubes *(upper right)*

With the Fastube and Fasturn, this beginner pillow is constructed quickly, using the Viking #1 decorative stitches between each row of tubes.

Product and fabric credits:
Fastube and Fasturn (The Crowning Touch Co.), Fairfield pillow form

Skill level: *Beginner*

Sandra Benfield
The Crowning Touch Co.

Shirred Fun *(middle right)*

This quick-to-make pillow utilizes iron-on shirring tape, covered buttons, and safety pins. I covered a pillow form with decorator fabric, then criss-crossed and saftey-pinned shirred companion strips around the pillow.

Product and fabric credits: *Dritz Iron-on Shirr-Rite Tape, Fairfield pillow form; Springs Industries fabric*

Skill level: *Beginner*

PHOTO COURTESY OF CHRIS BABICKE

Janis Bullis
Prym-Dritz Corporation (Pillow submitted by Dianne Giancola)

Quilted Neck Roll *(lower right)*

A neck roll pillow form is made from two layers of Fusible Fleece and Thermolam Plus. The cover is machine quilted following stripes and/or outline of flowers and leaves — an easy exercise for beginners.

Product and fabric credits:
Pellon Wonder-Under, Fusible Fleece, and Thermolam Plus

Skill level: *Beginner*

Jane Schenck
Manager, Education Fashion Services Freudenberg Nonwovens

Ruffled Bow *(lower left)*

Beginners can make this serged pillow. We used filler cord gathering with the flatlock stitch on the serger and wrapped corners.

Product and fabric credits: *Concord Fabrics by Joan Ressler; Fairfield pillow form*

Skill level: *Beginner*

Tammy Young
Freelance Author

Naomi Baker
Freelance Author

Dritz No-sew Sunflower *(upper left)*

Safety pins keep this beginner level, no-sew pillow together. A 35" (87.5cm) square of fabric is wrapped around a 14" (35cm) square pillow form envelope-style and safety pinned. Fabric for the button cover is accented with French knots, then button is covered. The ruffle around the sunflower button is made with a strip of fabric cut 3" × 25" (7.5cm × 63.5cm): long edges are pressed under 1/2" (1.3cm), then Shirr-Rite tape is ironed on the strip, which is shirred to 9" (23cm) on the inside and 13" (33cm) on the outside to create the flower petals.

Product and fabric credits: *Springs Industries fabric, Dritz Iron-on Shirr-Rite Tape, Fairfield pillow form*

Skill level: *Beginner*

Janis Bullis
*Prym-Dritz
Corporation
(Pillow submitted by
Dianne Giancola)*

Annie Tuley's Twisted Ribbon *(upper right)*

Use the Perfect Pleater and Annie Tuley's ribbon technique explained in her vest pattern to make this beginner project.

Product credit: *Annie Tuley's Honeycomb and Twisted Ribbon vest pattern, Wright ribbons*

Skill level: *Beginner*

Annie Tuley
*(no photo available)
(Pillow submitted
by Clotilde)*

Fabulous-Fur/Fabu-Leather *(middle right)*

This is a beginner level pillow. Two pieces of fabric are stitched right-sides together, turned, a pillow form inserted, and the opening hand-stitched closed.

Product and fabric credits: *Leopard Fabulous Fur, French vanilla Fabu-leather*

Skill level: *Intermediate*

Donna Salyers
*President,
Fabulous Fur*

Lion Pillow *(lower right)*

This pillow is made with two printed face cloths, sewn right-sides together around three sides, filled with loose fiberfill, then sewn shut by hand. On one side of the pillow, the lion's mane is textured by securing bunches of yarn to the lion's head. Variation: pad areas you wish and trapunto before sewing cloths together.

Product and fabric credits: *Simplicity, Simply the Best Home Decorating Book (collaborating author, Simon & Schuster, 1993) .*

Skill level: *Beginner*

Maureen Klein
Maureen Klein Creative Design Services Q & A columnist, "Sewing Decor" Editor, "Weekend Decorating Projects" ("Woman's Day" special interest publication)

Melissa's Pillow *(bottom)*

Pati Palmer's daughter, Melissa, created the pillow using the Winky Cherry book: *My First Embroidery Book, A Name Sampler* (Palmer/Pletsch Publishing). She used the squares in the gingham check as a guide to cross-stitch her name on this pillow.

Product and fabric credits: *Dan River Gingham*

Skill level: *Beginner*

Melissa Palmer
designer Winky Cherry, author/teacher Palmer/Pletsch Publishing

Pleated Churn Dash *(middle left)*

Annie Tuley cleverly used the Perfect Pleater to create the triangles in this pieced pillow square.

Product credit: *Fabric Traditions fabric, Perfect Pleater, Clotilde's fusible knit interfacing*

Skill level: *Intermediate*

Annie Tuley
(no photo available) (Pillow submitted by Clotilde)

Sources of Supplies

Please ask your sewing-machine or fabric dealer to order for you any product she or he doesn't stock. If you do not have access to a complete store, try mail order. As a courtesy, please include a self-addressed stamped envelope when inquiring. While we have tried to be accurate and complete, addresses change, businesses move or die, and we make regrettable omissions by mistake (advance apologies to anyone we left out). Please send updates to us in care of Open Chain Publishing, P.O. Box 2364-P, Menlo Park, CA 94026.

Air-Lite Synthetics Mfg., Inc.
342 Irwin Street
Pontiac, MI 48341-2982
Simplicity quilt batting, Fiberfil, pillow forms, urethane foam rolls, quilt batting on rolls, Comfort Fil 7 (Polargard) continuous filament batting, poly-insulate quilt batting.

Aleene's
Division of Artis, Inc.
Buellton, CA 93427
Glues, Stop Fraying, Tack-It.

Bernina of America, Inc.
3500 Thayer Court
Aurora, IL 60504-6182
Bernina and Bernette sewing machines and sergers, plus accessories.

Brother International Corp.
200 Cottontail Lane
Somerset, NJ 08875
Sewing machines and Homelock sergers.

Buffalo Batt & Felt Corp.
3307 Walden Avenue
Depew, NY 14043
Super Fluff fiberfill, batting.

Clotilde, Inc.
2 Sew Smart Way
Stevens Point, WI 54481-80301
Perfect Pleater pleater board, sewing notions catalog. Order line: (800) 772-2891.

CM Offray & Son, Inc.
P.O. Box 601
Chester, NJ 07930
Quality ribbons.

Coats & Clark
30 Patewood Drive, Suite 351
Greenville, SC 29615
Coats Dual Duty Plus for Overlock, Transparent Nylon Monofilament, Metallic, and Rayon threads plus Double Fold Bias Tape.

Concord House
1359 Broadway
New York, NY 10018
Multi-purpose fabrics for apparel, bridal, quilting, home decorating and crafts.

The Crowning Touch Inc.
2410 Glory C Road
Medford, OR 97501
Fasturn and Fastube Sewing Foot.

Dritz Corp.
P.O. Box 5028
Spartanburg, SC 29304
Stitch Witchery, Hem-N-Trim, Disappearing Ink Marking Pen, Fray Check, Sewing/Craft Glue Stick, Iron-On Drapery Tapes, and Shade-Maker.

Elna, Inc.
7642 Washington Avenue South
Eden Prairie, MN 55344
Elna and Elnita sewing machines and Elnalock sergers, Elnapress, Amazing Trace Embroiderer, notions, accessories, and Ribbon Thread.

Fabric Traditions
1350 Broadway
New York, NY 10018
Multi-purpose fabrics for apparel, quilting, home decorating and crafts.

Fabulous Fur
Donna Salyers
700 Madison Avenue
Covington, Kentucky 41011
Man-made furs and leather, sewing how-to books, videos, related patterns & notions. Free catalog.

Fairfield Processing Corp.
88 Rose Hill Avenue
P.O. Drawer 1157
Danbury, CT 06810
Products include four types of fiberfill (Poly-Fil, Poly-Fil Supreme, Crafter's Choice, and EZ Stuff), four bonded and two needlepunch battings in a variety of sizes, pillow forms in firm and down-like softness, pellets for use as weighted stuffing material, and a line of patterns. Call (800) 243-0989 for nearest retail store in your area.

Fiskars Manufacturing Corp.
7811 W. Stewart Avenue
Wausau, WI 54401
Rotary cutter with straight, pinking, and wave blades; cutting mats; and rulers.

Gingher, Inc.
P.O. Box 8865
Greensboro, NC 27419
Top-quality scissors, shears, and thread snips.

Global Village Imports
1101 SW Washington, Suite 140
Portland, OR 97205-2313
Handwoven 100% cotton fabrics and trim from Guatemala for apparel, home decorating, and quilting.

Gosling Tapes
1814 Marian Avenue
Thousand Oaks, CA 91360
Decorator tapes.

Gutermann of America, Inc.
8227 Arrowridge Boulevard
Charlotte, NC 28273
Hand and machine sewing threads; cone threads for sergers; heavy duty topstitching, metallic, silk, upholstery, and cotton quilting threads.

Handler Textile Corp.
24 Empire Boulevard
Moonachie, NJ 07074
Armo Weft, Touch 'O Gold, Rinseaway, Easy Stitch, Trans-Web Tape, Fuse-A-Shade, Fuse-A-Craft, and HTC Fusible Fleece.

Hoffman California Fabrics
25792 Obrero Drive
Mission Viejo, CA 92691
Fashion, quilting, decorator fabrics.

Hollywood Trims Inc.
42005 Cook Street
Palm Desert, CA 92260
Decorator trims and tassels.

JHB International Inc.
1955 S. Quince Street
Denver, CO 80231
Fashion, bridal, pearl, holiday, children's and men's blazer buttons; jewelry findings; eyes; charms; thimbles; sweetheart labels.

Juki America, Inc.
3555 Lomita Boulevard, Suite HI
Torrance, CA 90505
Jukilock sergers.

Kittrich
4500 District Boulevard
Los Angeles, CA 90058
Iron-on Clear Cover and self-adhesive vinyl and fabric decorative coverings.

S.H. Kunin Felt Co. Inc./Foss Mfg. Co.
380 LaFayette Road
Hampton, NH 03842-5000
Classic Rainbow Felt, Prestige Felt and Holiday Felt; Rainbow Plush Craft Fur; display fabric; Presto felt squares (just cut, peel, and stick); and Presto letters and numbers.

Madeira Marketing LTD
600 E. 9th Street
Michigan City, IN 46360
Decorative machine threads. (219) 873-1000.

Mill Creek Fabrics
295 Fifth Avenue
New York, NY 10016
Multi-purpose fabrics for apparel, home decorating, and crafts.

Morning Glory Products
P.O. Box 979
Taylor, TX 76574-6979
Batting and pillow forms.

Mundial Inc.
50 Kerry Place
Norwood, MA 02062
Appliqué scissors, embroidery scissors, and clippers.

Nancy's Notions, Ltd.
333 Beichl Avenue
Beaver Dam, WI 53916-0683
Specialty presser feet, adhesives, elastics, and sewing catalog.

New Home Sewing Machine
100 Hollister Road
Teterboro, NJ 07608
Sewing machines, Mylock sergers, specialty presser feet, and accessories. (201) 440-8080.

Pellon Division
Freudenberg Nonwovens
1040 Avenue of the Americas
New York, NY 10018
Wonder Under, Heavy-Duty Wonder Under, Sof-Shape, Easy-Knit, Stitch-n-Tear, Pellon Fusible Fleece, Decor-Bond, and Wonder Shade.

Pfaff Sewing Machine Co.
610 Winters Avenue
Paramus, NJ 07653
Pfaff sewing machines and Hobbylock sergers, PC Designer Software.

Quilters' Resource Inc.
P.O. Box 14885
Chicago, IL 60614
Silk prepleated ribbons, French ribbons, heirloom trim, antique buttons and embellishments, 100% silk thread, patterns, books, unusual notions.

Repcon International, Inc.
P.O. Box 548
Nixa, MO 65714
Infinity Rings, Fan-Decor, Frame-Decor, Garland-Decor, and Wreath-Decor.

Riccar America
c/o Tacony Corporation
1760 Gilsinn Lane
Fenton, MO 63026
Riccar sewing machines and sergers.

Rosebar Textile Co., Inc.
93 Entin Road
Clifton, NJ 07014
Elegant fabrics including satin.

Signature
P.O. Box 507
Mount Holly, NC 28120
All-Purpose and specialty threads, including Swiss Metrosene.

Singer Sewing Co.
135 Raritan Center Parkway
Edison, NJ 08837-3642
Singer sewing machines, Ultralock sergers, and Magic Steam Press.

Springs Industries
104 W. 40th Street
New York, NY 10018
Ultrasuede and related fabrics.

Sterns Technical Textiles Co.
100 Williams Street
Cincinnati, OH 45215
Mountain Mist battings.

Streamline Industries Inc.
845 Stewart Avenue
Garden City, NY 11530
Buttons, buckles, ribbons, ribbon bows, crests, appliqués.

Sulky of America
3113D Broadpoint Drive
Harbor Heights, FL 33983
Sulky rayon and metallic thread; Solvy water-soluble stabilizer; and Totally Stable.

Sullivans USA Inc.
224 Williams Street
Bensenville, IL 60106
Sullivans notions, adhesives, Fix Velour Hook and Loop Tape, zippers, Fray Stoppa.

Tacony Corp.
1760 Gilsinn Lane
Fenton, MO 63026
Baby Lock Sergers (Éclipse) and sewing machines (Ésanté); Simplicity sewing machines and sergers; Pattern-Life to reinforce and stabilize paper patterns; notions; books; and accessories.

June Tailor, Inc.
P.O. Box 208
Richfield, WI 53076
Rotary cutters, boards, mats, appliqué mat, pressing and ironing equipment. (800) 844-5400.

Tandy Leather Co.
P.O. Box 791
Fort Worth, TX 76101
Leather, suede, beads, laces, and patterns. Catalog $1.00.

Taylor Bedding
P.O. Box 979
Taylor, TX 76570-0979
Batting and pillow forms.

Therm O Web
770 Glenn Avenue
Wheeling, IL 60090
HeatnBond Original, HeatnBond Lite fusibles

Tinsel Threads, Inc.
Horn of America
P.O. Box 608
Sutton, WV 26601
Machine embroidery rayon and metallic threads.

V.I.P. Fabrics
1412 Broadway
New York, NY 10018
Multi-purpose fabrics for apparel, quilting, home decorating, and crafts.

VWS
11760 Berea Road
Cleveland, OH 44111
Viking and White sewing machines, Viking Huskylock sergers, White Superlock sergers, specialty presser feet, and accessories.

Windsor Oak Publishing
2043 E. Joppa Road, Suite 354
Baltimore, MD 21234
Publishers of Donna Babylon's book Pillow Pizzaz
(24 decorative pillows and many pillow-making techniques and one-of-a-kind styles).

Wm. E. Wright Ltd.
85 South Street
West Warren, MA 01092
Laces, trims, Woven Ribbons, Wire Edge Ribbons, Appliqués, Sequin Appliqués, Collars, Tapes and Braids, Bondex, Boye Needles.

YLI
482 N. Freedom Boulevard
Provo, UT 84601
Designer 6 decorative rayon thread, Woolly Plus heavy-weight wooly nylon thread, monofilament nylon thread, and Perfect Sew universal needle threader and needle inserter.

About the Authors

Jackie Dodson

Prolific author Jackie Dodson lives in a La Grange Park, Illinois, home stuffed with fabric, yarn, beads, books, sewing machines, sergers — and a patient husband. She earned a Bachelor of Arts degree from Carthage College and attended the University of Iowa and Wisconsin State Teachers' College. Previously employed as a high school teacher, Jackie is now a full-time writer and designer. She is the author or co-author of eleven books in the *Know Your Sewing Machine* series, co-author of *Gifts Galore,* author of *Twenty Easy Machine-Made Rugs, How to Make Soft Jewelry, Quick Quilted Home Decor with your Sewing Machine, Quick Quilted Home Decor with your Bernina Sewing Machine,* and co-author, with Jan Saunders, of *Sew & Serge Terrific Textures.*

She is a member of the following associations: Hinsdale Embroiderers' Guild; DuPage Textile Arts Guild; American Sewing Guild; Council of American Embroiderers; and Textile, Clothing, and Related Arts Forum. She has appeared on the popular *Sewing with Nancy* and *America Sews with Sue Hausmann* television programs and has written numerous magazine and newsletter articles, including regular columns for The American Sewing Guild in Chicago, The *Needlework Times,* and *The Creative Machine Newsletter.* Viking/Vogue recently featured her embellished vest in *Vogue Patterns* magazine and made a pattern available.

Jackie has also conducted lectures and seminars for guilds, sewing machine dealers, fabric stores, and national sewing and craft organizations.

In her spare time Jackie enjoys sewing for fun, and spending time with her family at their vacation home in northern Wisconsin.

After her guest semester at the New York Fashion Institute of Technology in New York City, Jan Saunders graduated with a B. A. in home economics, secondary education, and business from Adrian College, Adrian, Michigan. Saunders has spent the last 22 years sharing her flair for fashion and love for sewing with home sew-ers nationwide.

Formerly the education director of a major sewing machine company and of the largest fabric chain in the United States, this Swiss-trained specialist has handled company public relations, developed marketing plans and educational materials, written teaching curriculum and company newsletters, and conducted sales training and sewing seminars nationwide. As the former National Program Director for the Sew Better Seminars program, Jan managed a national team of sewing and serging specialists who taught fashion sewing, serging, wearable art, and home decorating seminars to consumers across the country.

Jan Saunders

In 1980, her first book, *Speed Sewing* became a Book-of-the-Month selection. Since then she has written the best-selling *Sew, Serge, Press* (Chilton, 1989), and the *Teach Yourself to Sew Better* four-book series (Chilton, 1990 - 1993). In her most recent book, *Jan Saunders' Wardrobe Quick-Fixes* (Chilton, 1995), she shares industry secrets and offers readers quick practical suggestions on how to embellish, repair, and care for their clothing. Jan has also co-authored *Sew & Serge Terrific Textures* with Jackie Dodson, due out this year. Also look for Jan's regular contributions to *Serger Update, Sewing Update, The Creative Machine Newsletter, Sew News,* and *Threads* and her guest appearances on *America Sews with Sue Hausmann* and *The Sew Perfect Show* with Sandra Betzina.

In her spare time, Jan enjoys sewing for pleasure, sailing, cross-country and downhill skiing, classical music, and spending time with her husband Ted, and son Todd.

Index